ONE DAY WON

BIBLE ACTIVITY EVENTS FOR CHILDRI

Author: Tamar Pollard
Series Editor: Alison Mitchell

CONTENTS

The small print

One Day Wonders: Christmas, Easter, Halloween

© The Good Book Company 2010

ISBN: 9781907377259

Original material written by Tamar Pollard. Edited by Alison Mitchell (alison@thegoodbook.co.uk).

Published by The Good Book Company, 37 Elm Road, New Malden, Surrey, KT3 3HB, UK. admin@thegoodbook.co.uk Tel: 0333 123 0880. Int: +44 (0) 20 8942 0880

UK: www.thegoodbook.co.uk   **N America:** www.thegoodbook.com   **Australia:** www.thegoodbook.com.au   **New Zealand:** www.thegoodbook.co.nz

Bible verses taken from the HOLY BIBLE, NEW INTERNATIONAL VERSION, copyright © 1973, 1978, 1984 International Bible Society. Used by permission.

Designs by Wild Associates Ltd and Jon Bradley. Cover by André Parker. Extra illustrations by Kirsty McAllister. Printed in the UK.

thegoodbook
COMPANY

INTRODUCTION TO ONE DAY WONDERS

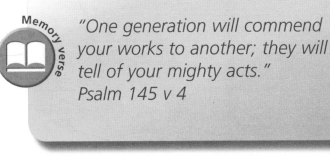

Memory verse

"One generation will commend your works to another; they will tell of your mighty acts."
Psalm 145 v 4

Notes for leaders

It is so exciting to think that on the doorstep of every church is a community waiting to be reached with the gospel. As Psalm 145 reminds us, children's and families' work should be an integral part of this evangelism. Running special events for these groups provides us with brilliant and unique opportunities to:

* make contact with people who would never usually set foot in church.

* build relationships.

* impact many with the good news of Jesus.

One Day Wonders provides you with three complete seasonal events, suitable for churched and unchurched children. Within each are three alternative session formats, including one aimed at whole families.

The idea is that they can be used as stand-alone events, and yet, at the same time, slot into your church's programme for outreach and your regular children's groups. You may opt to use the event as a holiday-club or vacation Bible school reunion or in place of a holiday club; as an extension to your weekly clubs; or as a one-

off special in a local school. Once you have determined your aims (see page 6), flexibility is the name of the game!

There is a diverse range of activities in *One Day Wonders*, allowing to you to pick'n'mix challenges, games, crafts, refreshments and songs, to go alongside your central Bible-teaching slot. Some activities are there simply to help children get to know you and "let off steam", whereas others are intentionally designed to consolidate the main teaching point (the "big idea") of the event. It is worth noting that the small-group material is differentiated for different age groups (4-7s, 7-9s, and 9-11s).

Note: This book contains a number of photocopiable pages, including planning sheets, permission forms, small-group material and craft activities. All of these photocopiables can also be downloaded for free (including some full-colour options) from the following websites:

UK: www.thegoodbook.co.uk/onedaywonders
N America: www.thegoodbook.com/onedaywonders
Australia: www.thegoodbook.com.au/onedaywonders
New Zealand: www.thegoodbook.co.nz/onedaywonders

HOW TO USE THIS BOOK

BIBLE PASSAGE: All sessions are Bible-focused.

Aim

The aim is the "big idea" taught during the session. It is Bible-based and child-oriented.

This verse is usually based on the NIV Bible and will be taught during the children's events.

Notes for leaders

Based on the Bible passage

Notes for leaders give Bible context and background to the passage.

Event options

Each event has a choice of three options: a short event for children, a longer event for children (sometimes with an opportunity to invite adults along for the end section), and a family event.

The summary page allows you to quickly compare the options and choose the most suitable one for your target audience. Once you have decided upon your event format, the planning sheets further unpack the events and leave space for you to personalise the outline with your selection of activities and team members involved.

The timings in each are merely a guide and, as the co-ordinator, you will need to consider what will work best in your context.

Teaching time

There are two suggested talks for each event, one for the "children-only" event and one that can be used either at the family event or the "children-only" event. The talks make the "big idea" clear and memorable, and have applications that are closely connected, age-appropriate and specific. They are faithful to the passage and are visual and accessible, aiming to help those we're working with to engage with the Bible passage.

What the leader actually says to the children is shown in bold type. Directions to the leaders are in normal type.

Small groups

The small-group material is age-specific and is based on the passage being taught. Running such groups provides the opportunity to consolidate the teaching, as well as allowing children the chance to ask questions and build relationships with the team members (see pages 8-9 for further information on leading small groups).

Ideas menu

Each session has an **Ideas Menu**, which includes a suggestion on how you can teach the memory verse, an idea for teaching about prayer and some song suggestions. The music suggested is on readily available CDs (available from The Good Book Company www.thegoodbook.co.uk).

In addition there is a range of team challenges, crafts, games and other activities to choose from, to suit your event and the time you have available.

Supplies for crafts and games can be found online. Helpful websites include www.bakerross.co.uk in the UK or www.orientaltrading.com in N America.

TIMETABLE FOR PUTTING ON AN EVENT

Time	Activity	✔	Leader
	Tick when materials are ready for each activity		
Four months or more before the event	Decide if you want it to be an event for children or families, and if you will have any follow-up events afterwards.		
	Set the date and check it doesn't clash with anything important (either within the church or local schools).		
	Chat to your church leadership about your aims and how they fit in with the church's vision and programme. Check that they are in support of the event.		
Three months or more before the event	Publicise dates to congregation and think about how many team members you're needing to recruit.		
	Consider long-term craft preparation (eg: what resources do you need the congregation to be saving?).		
	Decide what ages you are going to offer the event to and if you will split it down into smaller age groups.		
	Decide how you are going to promote the event in schools / at church.		
Two months or more before the event	Open meeting of interested individuals. Ensure your church's child protection policy is followed for everyone offering to join the team.		
	Estimate attendance.		
	Order any materials you need for the crafts, games etc.		
	Compile a registration list.		
	Send the publicity to print.		
One week before the event	Decorations		
	Check supplies.		
On the day!	Arrive early. Take time for prayer.		
	Watch for any rough patches that need adjustment (eg: timings that need to be altered or asking team members to sit with any unsettled children).		
	After the children leave, have a brief team meeting to tie up any loose ends.		
Week after the event	"Thank you's" to the team.		
	Review evaluations and suggestions from team.		
	Photo display for congregation (let them know what they missed).		
	Write to non-church families, reminding them about other upcoming events or regular church-based clubs.		

AIMS

The events will provide enjoyable, imaginative and controllable ways of sharing the good news of Jesus with children and families in your neighbourhood. All of these events seek to teach about the love of God and our need to respond to His offer of salvation. In addition, each event will have specific aims stated at the start of each section.

Alongside these broader aims, you will need to decide what your particular aims for the event are, such as:

- to present the gospel to children who have never really heard it.

- to renew contact and further develop links after a holiday club or vacation Bible school.

- to launch a new regular children's group.

- to attract new children to join your church's Sunday groups or midweek activities.

- to deepen your relationships with children you already work with.

- to provide an opportunity for children to make a commitment to Christ.

- to encourage the children in your church groups to be reaching out to their friends.

- to develop your relationships with families connected in some way to the church.

It may be helpful to work through the concentric circles below to establish which your primary aims are and how you will be able to evaluate the event afterwards to see if they were met. The purpose of the circles is to show the different stages we go through in our evangelism and discipleship. It is useful to consider which main stage your event is targeted at and the next stage you are aiming for.

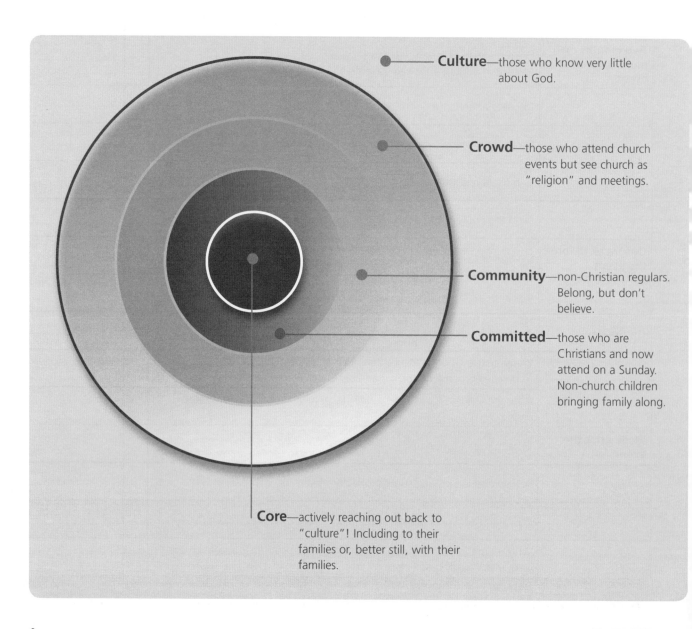

Culture—those who know very little about God.

Crowd—those who attend church events but see church as "religion" and meetings.

Community—non-Christian regulars. Belong, but don't believe.

Committed—those who are Christians and now attend on a Sunday. Non-church children bringing family along.

Core—actively reaching out back to "culture"! Including to their families or, better still, with their families.

TEAM RECRUITMENT AND TRAINING

Recruiting

The team you recruit is an essential part of the work. The minimum recommended adult-to-child ratios are as follows:

- 1:8—for children aged three-eight years.
- 1:12—for children aged eight and over.

Within the team, there will be a whole range of roles that need filling. It is not essential that all the workers are experienced children's workers, for many others in your church will be more than able to help in the kitchen, on registration and in other background areas. Others will be capable of running small-group sessions after some initial basic training. Serving together is a fantastic way of developing relationships within the church and allowing different people's gifts to be used, including teenagers.

Before you start recruiting your team, make sure you have looked through your church's child protection policy. All leaders involved should fill in and sign a confidential declaration form (see page 12 for a sample UK form) stating whether or not they have been the subject of criminal or civil proceedings, and whether they have caused harm to any child or put them at risk. Emphasise to your team that this is the requirement of legal best-practice—but in addition, as Christians, we should respect the law of the land (Titus 3 v 1), we should be above reproach (1 Timothy 3 v 7), and our willingness to be checked is part of our commitment to care for the children. If anyone gives an answer that causes concern, allow them to explain this disclosure personally. If you are in any doubt, consult your church leader. You may also find it useful to ask for a brief reference as part of the process. Ensure that confidentiality is maintained throughout.

Training

It is really important to meet with your team in the weeks leading up to the event, to run through the event's aims, child protection issues and different roles, as well as to provide basic training.

Suggested agenda:

- Icebreaker and introductions.
- Short devotion and prayer.
- Share the aims of the event, including where it fits into the bigger picture of church ministry and evangelism.
- The legal stuff—child protection (summarise your church policy), health and safety, and emergency procedures.
- The event's format and timings.
- Roles—both specific (see pages 9-10) and general guidelines on befriending children and being good role models (see below).
- Training on good behaviour management, running small groups and how to counsel children.
- Prayer.

Being a good role model	
DOs	**DON'Ts**
Do learn their names quickly, use them and pray for them.	**Don't** have any favourites.
Do get to know the children as individuals—pay attention to the way they act, react and interact.	**Don't** be on your own with just one child.
Do look out for the loners and shy ones.	**Don't** be tactile with them. Touch should be related to the child's needs, not the worker's. It should be age-appropriate and generally initiated by the child, rather than the worker, eg: when the child is in distress or needs medical attention.
Do be patient, positive, kind and enthusiastic.	**Don't** pressurise a child into making a commitment to Christ (more on that later).
Do be consistent in your expectations and firm in your ground rules.	**Don't** label them (eg: as "good", "difficult", "is / is not obviously a Christian")
Do be clear in your instructions.	**Don't** stand around chatting to other leaders—your priority is the children.
Do be confident and creative in your delivery—adapt the material and your choice of vocabulary to suit your group and yourself.	**Don't** forget to prepare.
Do use body language, eye contact and voice intonation to help keep attention.	**Don't** be afraid to ask for help.

Good behaviour management

Discipline and control creates a truly relaxed, enjoyable and reverent environment within which we can communicate the message of the gospel, both through our own Christ-like actions and through the material we teach. Good relationships and clear expectations are at the heart of loving, effective discipline.

It may be useful to have a signal or set phrase with accompanying action that your team members can use when you want the children to stop what they are doing and be silent.

In addition, a step-by-step approach to behaviour management can help, both when the children are all together and in smaller activity groups. For example:

1. **Watch for the children that wind others up and intervene before there is a problem.** Make intervention precise and clear, eg: "spread out and look out"—sitting among a group or separating certain groups of children.

2. **Try to use implicit cues** (ie: body language and eye contact) first. Always consider how, why and when you need to draw attention to misbehaviour.

3. **"Tell off" the individuals discreetly.** Be quiet, firm, precise and brief. Explain why they have not reached your expectations.

4. If the child alters their behaviour for the better, respond positively. If they do not, **offer the child a choice of improving their behaviour or taking time out**. Avoid threats you cannot carry out.

5. **If time out is taken, child to be seated for five minutes in lobby, with the worker** (ideally, out of sight of the other children, but make sure you can be seen by at least one other team member). There **hold a brief discussion as to what is at the heart of the problem, to get beyond the behaviour**. Use this to teach about repentance, eg: "If you come back and say sorry, then all will be forgiven and forgotten. We love you but your behaviour is unacceptable." Tailor your reprimand to the individual and occasion. **Note the date, child's name and behaviour in the incident book** (kept with the registration material).

6. **If a child has time out twice in the event**, their parents ought to be contacted. If persistent bad behaviour occurs, or if the safety of others cannot be guaranteed, then, as an ultimate sanction, the child must be excluded from the event.

When dealing with bad behaviour, it is important to:

- distinguish between those who are *distracting* (which is accidental eg: doing their shoelace) and those who are being *disruptive* (which is deliberate eg: un-doing someone else's shoelace).

- similarly, judge between *irresponsibility* (eg: the silly, thoughtless comment) and *defiance* (eg: the deliberate, opposite action).

- combine firmness with understanding. Recognise the difference between wrong-doing (stealing, lying, disobedience, insolence etc) and naughtiness—which may be caused by tiredness, illness or other problems. Encourage the children to identify the problem and think how they can resolve it.

- consider physical factors eg: the room, the weather, poor resources.

- remember there may be personality clashes, difficulties at home or upset through an unfamiliar routine.

- adapt to those with special needs eg: educational, behavioural or medical needs.

Running small groups

Small groups are a key element of an event, since it's often within them that relationships with leaders and children are built, and meaningful conversations can be had. For that reason, it is advisable to have one or two leaders to eight children to lead a group and work through a sheet. Where possible, the gender of the leaders should reflect the nature of the group.

When leading these times, keep in mind the DOs and DON'Ts on the next page.

Running small groups	
DOs	DON'Ts
Do ask questions that deal with feelings as well as facts eg: "How do you feel?"	**Don't** ask yes/no questions.
Do encourage honesty always.	**Don't** dismiss any contributions.
Do ask direct questions sometimes—be willing to challenge if appropriate.	**Don't** feel you have to answer everything.
Do ask questions that are relevant and at the right level.	**Don't** ask many questions based on prior knowledge.
Do follow up responses with more questions.	**Don't** do all the talking.
Do prepare and be prepared to be flexible.	**Don't** be afraid of silence.

How to counsel children

Pointing a child to Christ and giving them a clear opportunity to respond to the gospel message is plainly one of the most important parts of our work with children. It is crucial therefore that we know what to do when a child does respond.

When a child (or children) comes for counselling, find a quiet spot BUT DO NOT TAKE THEM INTO A DIFFERENT ROOM.

Find out why they want to speak to you. This can be quite revealing and helps you plan your approach: Because a friend came? To get a booklet? They don't know! Observe their expressions and body language, as well as their words. Do they seem serious or are they just messing about?

A child may have made some commitment before and be looking for assurance. This is part of their spiritual progress. Other times, we will simply be leading them one step further. Praise God if you lead them that last step, but remember there can be no last step without all the steps before. Every move towards Christ can be described as a "decision towards Christ". People don't just drift into a saving relationship with God in Christ. It involves decision, but it may, and probably does, involve a number of decisions.

Ask the child why they want to become a Christian. Impress on them that they must not do it only to please you but explain that you would be delighted if they did. It is helpful to go through a counselling booklet with them such as *Who will be King?* (available from The Good Book Company), as it guides their thoughts and is something for them to take away afterwards.

Use simple language without being childish and don't assume anything. Avoid jargon like "sin", "crucified" and "resurrection".

Explain that to become a Christian we need to make a response. You could use the pattern "sorry", "thank you", "please" for the prayer of commitment. "Sorry for all the wrong things I have done", "Thank you for dying in my place on the cross", "Please forgive me and change me and be King of my life". To ensure that a child has really understood, get them to tell you what they have to do. If they have not grasped it, explain again.

Explain the cost of commitment, putting Christ first and the need to stand up for what they believe. Explain also the need for fellowship, Bible reading and prayer in simple terms. Encourage them to tell their parents. Suggest they go away and think about it before praying, and then come back and tell you if they did. However, you can offer them the option of praying with you there and then. Don't pressurise.

Team Roles

Here are the roles you will need to delegate if you are running an event specifically for children:

- **Leaders-in-charge / Team captains**

These people co-ordinate the upfront leading of the event and keep everything to time. They need to be enthusiastic, flexible yet aware of the order, and authoritative.

- **Small-group leaders**

The role of the majority of the team is to sit among the children during the teaching sessions, to help enthuse and to keep order. However their key role is later as they accompany a small group of children in Bible discussion times, crafts and games sessions. They will have a great opportunity to get to know the children, have meaningful discussions about the teaching programme, and show the love of Christ in the way they act. It is therefore useful to allocate different leaders to the various age groups.

- **Musicians**

You may want a small band to play; otherwise you will need a couple of people who are confident singers to teach your songs to the children, using a CD. Singing is an enjoyable way to fix good words and biblical truths in the children's minds quickly. Encourage your team to join in any actions, as the children will only be as enthusiastic as the team are!

- **Memory-verse teacher**

Each session has a memory verse linked to it, along with a suggestion of how the verse can be taught. Since the verses will help the children understand the Bible and God's purposes for them, the person who is teaching it needs to include a clear and concise explanation, repetition, actions or visual cues.

- **Quiz leaders**

A quiz time in any programme should be seen as fun and enjoyable, but also a key part of the overall teaching programme, so...

   questions should reinforce main points of the story, as well as having a couple of questions on the verse and songs.

   there needs to be variety in the way the questions are asked (eg: Factual—who, what, why, when, where, how?; Multiple choice—make all possibilities plausible; Matching pairs—give the missing one; True or false; Complete the verse / fill in the missing word).

   a range of children need to be asked and their answers repeated so all can hear.

   be fair—make sure that each team's questions are of the same level of difficulty. Explain the rules and stick to them (eg: how many chances a team gets).

   be exciting—encourage quick answers and cheering.

- **Registration team**

This team will be responsible for ensuring every child is registered and welcomed, as well as seeking to build links with the parents/guardians. You may also allocate one of them to stay at the desk throughout the event to keep an eye on latecomers, site security and the collection of the children at the end of the event.

A register also needs to be kept of the leaders present. These records must be retained for seven years.

- **Refreshment team**

The team is responsible for preparing the refreshments for the children (and families if you are running something for parents also); checking with the registration team if any children have food allergies; and tidying up after the refreshments have been distributed.

- **First aider**

Appoint at least one member of your team to be the official first aider. These people will need a current first-aid certificate and access to the first-aid kit. Kept with the first-aid kit should be an accident/incident book and it is essential that records are kept. Make sure all the team know who the first aider is, along with any emergency procedures.

Non-essentials:

- **Kit man**

This person will be responsible for setting up any TV or projector equipment and public address system that is required.

- **Craft team/person**

While most of the team will help out in their allocated age group's craft time, you may find it useful to appoint someone to be responsible for planning the craft activities, and making sure all the resources needed are in the correct place, at the correct time.

- **Timekeeper**

This person needs to sit towards the front and hold up time signs to show those leading how long there is to go. They also play an essential role when group work is going on as they enable everyone to work in tandem.

- **Scorekeepers**

Keep track of any points awarded.

- **Point givers**

Points can be used as incentives. Children can be awarded them for sitting quietly, answering a question, singing enthusiastically etc. If they are used, it is important to make sure lots are distributed evenly by those sat among the children.

PUBLICITY

Once you have decided on your event and timings, and have started the team recruitment process, the next big thing to work on is making sure children come! There are ideas below for publicising each event (these can be downloaded from the websites below). If you are designing your own publicity, then make sure it is visually attractive and the following things are clear:

- Who is running the event.

- When, where and at what time the event is on.

- Which ages the event is for.

- What sort of activities are on offer.

- If there is a cost.

- Who to contact for further information.

Who you are aiming at will determine the amount of publicity you produce as well as your distribution of publicity. Schools are often willing to give out invitations—and even more likely if you put the invitations into class sets of thirty! It is also useful to give them to the schools in advance so they have plenty of time to pass them on to the children.

Some schools may be happy for you to run a promotional assembly, especially those schools where your church already has contacts. If you do have an assembly slot, be sure to find out how long it should last, as well as making it as creative as you can—you want something to whet the children's appetite.

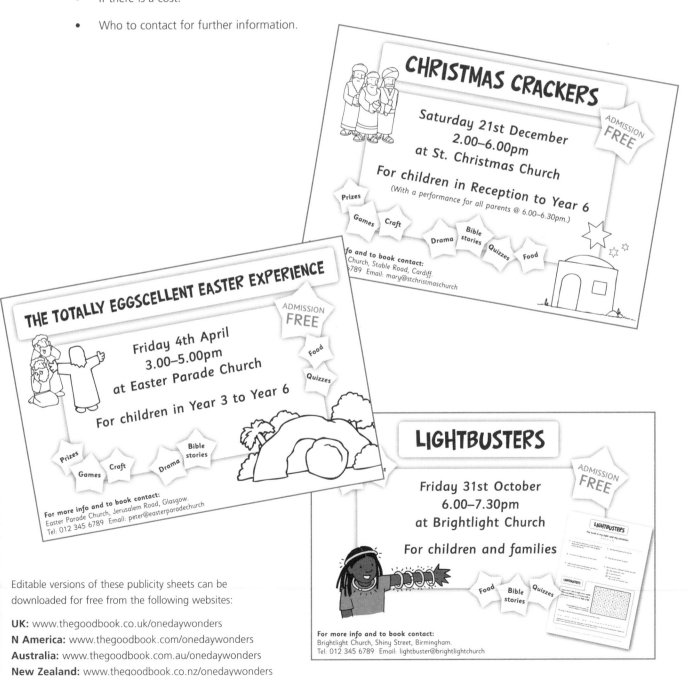

Editable versions of these publicity sheets can be downloaded for free from the following websites:

UK: www.thegoodbook.co.uk/onedaywonders
N America: www.thegoodbook.com/onedaywonders
Australia: www.thegoodbook.com.au/onedaywonders
New Zealand: www.thegoodbook.co.nz/onedaywonders

Confidential Declaration Form

In the UK, guidelines from the Home Office following the Children Act 1989 advise that all voluntary organisations, including churches, take steps to safeguard the children who are in their care. You are therefore asked to make the following declarations.

Because of the nature of the work for which you are applying, this post is exempt from the provision of section 4(ii) of the Rehabilitation of Offenders Act 1974, by virtue of the Rehabilitation of Offenders Act 1974 (exemptions) Orders 1975, and you are therefore not entitled to withhold information about convictions which, for other purposes, are "spent" under the provisions of the Act. In the event of an appointment, any failure to disclose such convictions could result in the withdrawal of approval to work with children in the church.

Do you have any current or spent criminal convictions, cautions, bindovers or cases pending?

Yes   No

Have you ever been held liable by a court under the Rehabilitation of Offenders Act 1974 for a civil wrong, or had an order made against you by a matrimonial or family court?

Yes   No

Has your conduct ever caused, or been likely to harm a child or put a child at risk, or, to your knowledge, has it ever been alleged that your conduct has resulted in any of these things?

Yes   No

Signed _____   Date _____

Referee's Name:

Referee's Address:

Referee's Telephone: Referee's Email:

Registration and Parental Consent Form

Name of child _____ Date of birth _____

Name of child _____ Date of birth _____

Name of child _____ Date of birth _____

Address:

Postcode:

Email:

Phone: Mobile:

Name(s) of parent / guardian:

School your child attends:

Please give details of any health problems, medical conditions or allergies affecting your child, or any medication that they may be taking.

Please give any other information that you think may be useful to us in caring for your child:

To be read and signed by a parent / guardian:

☐ I give permission for my son / daughter to take part. I understand that leaders will take all reasonable care during the club, but I acknowledge the possibility that my child, for a short time, may be out of sight of a leader during the club time. I understand that personal accident insurance is my responsibility. I give permission for emergency medical treatment to be carried out in the event that I cannot be contacted.

☐ I am happy for my details to be kept on a church database, to be informed of other events.

☐ I give permission for photographs / video to be taken of my child for internal use only.

Signed _____ Date _____

CHRISTMAS CRACKERS

MATTHEW 1 v 18-25; 2 v 1-18; LUKE 1 v 26-38; 2 v 1-20

Aim

To help the children (and their families if it's a family event) to:

▶ know that Jesus is God's Son
▶ understand that Jesus came at Christmas to be our Saviour.

Memory verse

The Father has sent his Son to be the Saviour of the world. 1 John 4 v 14 (NIV)

Notes for leaders

 Read **Matthew 1 v 18-25; 2 v 1-18; Luke 1 v 26-38; 2 v 1-20.**

Our main sources for the Christmas narratives are taken from the Gospels of Matthew and Luke. As we read through these accounts, there is a wide range of information about Jesus to take on board:

- He's God Himself come to earth (**Matthew 1 v 23**).
- He's born of a virgin (**Matthew 1 v 18, 23, 25; Luke 1 v 34**).
- He's a real human like you and me.
- He's the promised Son of David (**Matthew 1 v 17; Luke 1 v 32**).
- He's God's eternal King (**Matthew 2 v 6; Luke 1 v 32-33**).
- He's the Son of God (**Matthew 2 v 15; Luke 1 v 32, 35**).
- He's the Saviour of the world (**Matthew 1 v 21; Luke 2 v 11**).

The Old Testament references littered throughout support these claims and are a helpful reminder of God's eternal salvation plan (**see Micah 5 v 2; Hosea 11 v 1; Jeremiah 31 v 11; Isaiah 7 v 14**). So are the wise men's gifts and all that they symbolised: gold, a gift for a king; frankincense, a fragrance that would have been used in the temple as a symbol of prayer, showing Jesus was God; myrrh, aromatic gum used in the treatment of dead bodies, and a reminder that Jesus had come to die. And so, the writers are making Jesus' divinity as clear as possible, as they long for their readers to grasp His identity and mission, and believe in Him.

It is always a challenge to apply this to our response to the good news. Do we believe that Jesus is fully human and therefore is our perfect mediator? Do we believe that Jesus is the Son of God? Do we believe that Jesus is King for ever, reigning supreme in all circumstances? Do we believe that God can do the impossible—at any time? And how can we communicate these truths of Jesus' identity and mission clearly to those we are working with, so that they grasp the truth of the first Christmas, and believe?

The example of Mary and Joseph and the way they trusted in God's word (**Matthew 1 v 24; Luke 1 v 38**); the joy of the shepherds and the way they shared their discovery (**Luke 2 v 16-20**); and the devotion of the wise men (**Matthew 2 v 2, 11**), are in sharp contrast to the hostility of Herod (**Matthew 2 v 13-16**) and the indifference of the priests (**Matthew 2 v 5-6**). These different characters' responses to the identity of Jesus, which run throughout the narrative, are reflective of the attitudes we will come across with those we are working with, and helpful for our application of the passage.

 Pray

Leader's prayer

Father God, we praise You and thank You for sending Jesus to be the Saviour of the world. As we seek to teach Your salvation plan, we pray that we would be those who trust in Your word and rejoice in Your goodness; that we would be those who clearly communicate Christ's identity and mission; and that those we are working with would not be hostile or indifferent, but rather, understand and believe.

Programme Options

Christmas is a time when many people, both young and old, will happily venture into church. The range of options below allows you to choose an event to reach local children, family groups or the wider community. The **"Aims"** section on page 6 gives help in deciding who you want to reach out to.

It is probably best to run your event in early December because:

- this ensures the children aren't too tired.
- an activity session gives parents valuable Christmas-shopping time.
- volunteers in your church are less likely to be busy elsewhere.

- it allows you to promote forthcoming Christmas events, such as carol services.

Once you have decided upon your target audience, choose an outline from the three options below. Then select games, crafts, challenges etc (see **Ideas Menu**, pages 25-30) and delegate accordingly.

The tables on the next three pages give you further details about each of the three suggested options for a Christmas event. Space is included to add the name of the team member responsible for each activity. You may find it helpful to give copies of this table to each member of your team. You can photocopy this page or download a copy for free from **www.thegoodbook.co.uk/onedaywonders**

Option A: Two-hour children's event

15 min	Registration and opening games (begins 10 min before start time)
25 min	Together Time 1—songs, team challenges, memory verse, quiz
25 min	Themed crafts (with drinks break)
25 min	Together Time 2—songs, team challenges, Bible story, prayer, quiz
15 min	Small groups
25 min	Themed games

Option B: Four-hour children's event
with parents invited to come and watch a half-hour performance afterwards

15 min	Registration and opening games (begins 10 min before start time)
25 min	Together Time 1—songs, team challenges, "Eyewitness 1", prayer
25 min	Themed crafts (with drinks break)
25 min	Together Time 2—songs, team challenges, "Eyewitness 2", quiz (1)
25 min	Themed games
25 min	Together Time 3—songs, team challenges, "Eyewitness 3", memory verse
40 min	Younger children watch Christmas DVD, older children rehearse play and some make props
25 min	Together Time 4—songs, team challenges, "Eyewitness 4", quiz (2)
20 min	Small groups
25 min	Food, final set-up and prizes
30 min	Performance—parents come and watch songs, verse and play

Option C: One-and-a-half-hour family fun event

10 min	Themed wall quiz and nativity signature bingo as families arrive
45 min	Games: Split everyone into four teams and run a number of games that aim to include everyone and require a mixture of skills eg: rapidough, snowball fight, ice-cube race and snowmen.
15 min	Festive refreshments and quiz
5 min	Children to sing
10 min	Talk
5 mins	Prizes

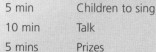

Option A: Two-hour children's event

2 Christmas Fun

Gear

- Name labels and pens
- Registration forms
- Colouring sheets and pencils
- Materials for your choice of games, challenges and crafts
- Visual aids for the Bible story
- Memory-verse props
- Music and words for songs
- Quiz questions and scoreboard
- Small-group sheets and pencils for each child
- Prizes
- Refreshments
- Publicity for Christmas services or events

Time	Activity	✔	Leader
	Tick when materials are ready for each activity		
Before event	Preparation eg: decorate the room, get crafts ready etc		
One hour before	Team meeting for prayer and final instructions		
10 minutes before (for 15 minutes)	Children arrive, register and are given a name label—before being taken to their opening activities eg: colouring competition, bouncy castle, opening games (see **Ideas Menu** for Christmas games, pages 28-30)		
25 minutes Together Time 1	Welcome—introduction of leaders, what's going to happen, rules etc Team challenge (see **Ideas Menu**, page 25) Song (see **Music spot**, page 25 for song suggestions) Team Challenge Memory verse (see **Ideas Menu**, page 25) Song Quiz (see **Ideas Menu**, page 26)		
25 minutes	Crafts (see **Ideas Menu**, pages 26-27) Drink and a snack in groups		
25 minutes Together Time 2	Team Challenge Song Bible story (**Talk idea 1**, page 20) Song Prayer (see **Ideas Menu**, page 28) Quiz		
15 minutes	Small-groups time (see **Ideas Menu**, page 28)		
25 minutes	Games (see **Ideas Menu**, pages 28-30)—maybe do one big game all together at the end. Promote upcoming events and award any prizes.		

Option B: Four-hour children's event

with parents invited to come and watch a half-hour performance afterwards

Gear

- Registration forms, name labels and pens
- Colouring sheets and pencils
- Materials for your games, challenges and crafts
- Visual aids for the Eyewitness accounts
- Memory verse-props
- Small-groups sheets and pencil for each child

- Music and words for songs
- Quiz questions and scoreboard
- Refreshments
- DVD player and screen
- Copies of play scripts
- Publicity for Christmas services or events

Time	Activity	✔	Leader
	Tick when materials are ready for each activity		
Before event	Preparation eg: decorate room, get crafts ready etc		
One hour before	Team meeting for prayer and final instructions		
10 minutes before (for 15 minutes)	Children arrive, register and are given a name label—before being taken to their opening activities eg: colouring competition, bouncy castle, opening games (see **Ideas Menu** for Christmas games, pages 28-30)		
25 minutes Together Time 1	Welcome—introduction of leaders, what's going to happen, rules etc Team challenge (see **Ideas Menu**, page 25) Song (see **Music Spot**, page 25) Team challenge Eyewitness 1—Mary (see page 22) Prayer (see **Ideas Menu**, page 28) Song		
25 minutes	Crafts (see **Ideas Menu**, pages 26-27) Drink and a snack in groups		
25 minutes Together Time 2	Team challenges Song Eyewitness 2—Joseph (see page 22) Team challenge Song Quiz (see **Ideas Menu**, page 26)		
25 minutes	Games (see **Ideas Menu**, pages 28-30)—Maybe do one big game all together at the end. Give details about church groups and invite children to come.		
25 minutes Together Time 3	Team challenge Song Memory verse (see **Ideas Menu**, page 25) Team challenge Eyewitness 3—Shepherds (see page 23) Song		
40 minutes	Younger children watch a Christmas DVD (see **Ideas Menu**, page 28) Older children rehearse their play (scripts on pages 36-38) *Optional: some children to bake mince pies or small cakes and make props. Alternatively, this could be done in the earlier craft session.*		
25 minutes Together Time 4	Team Challenges Song Eyewitness 4—Wise men (see page 23) Team Challenge Song Quiz		
20 minutes	Small groups (see **Ideas Menu**, page 28)		
25 minutes	Lunch/tea (You may provide something simple eg: hot dogs, crisps/chips, fruit, biscuits/cookies; alternatively your publicity could mention bringing sandwiches.) Towards the end, award prizes and play a quick game with those who have finished.		
30 minutes	Performance—parents come to see "It's a kind of Magi", along with the memory verse and songs. Light refreshments served. Announcements for other upcoming events.		

ONE DAY WONDERS

Option C: One-and-a-half-hour family fun event

Gear

- Nativity signature bingo sheets and pens
- Materials for your choice of games, challenges and crafts
- Visual aids for the talk
- Wall quiz
- Quiz questions and scoreboard
- Music and words for carol
- Refreshments
- Team posters (eg: Puddings, Crackers, Stars, Trees)
- Prizes
- Publicity for Christmas services or events

Time	Activity	✔	Leader
	Tick when materials are ready for each activity		
Before event	Preparation eg: decorate room, get games and refreshments ready etc		
One hour before	Team meeting for prayer and final instructions		
10 minutes before (for 15 minutes)	Doors open Nativity signature bingo (see **Ideas Menu**, page 28) Superstars wall quiz (see **Ideas Menu**, page 30)		
3 minutes	Introduction; then split entire group into 4 or 6 teams. All teams compete at the same time, one team per game. Every 7 minutes each team moves on to their next game. Try to choose a variety of games that will include everyone and need a range of skills. The following are suggestions. You may want to replace some or all with other games from pages 28-30.		
7 minutes	Nativity scavenger hunt (see **Ideas Menu**, page 29)		
7 minutes	Build a snowman, Father Christmas and Christmas tree (see **Ideas Menu**, "Snowmen and some!", page 28)		
7 minutes	Snowball fight (see **Ideas Menu**, page 28)		
7 minutes	Ice-cube race (see **Ideas Menu**, page 30)		
7 minutes	Rapidough (see **Ideas Menu**, page 28)		
7 minutes	Ski-ing plank race (see **Ideas Menu**, page 30)		
15 minutes	Festive refreshments eg: mince pies or small cakes, yule logs, turkey baguettes Quiz (see **Ideas Menu**, page 26)		
5 minutes	Song: either children who are linked with the church sing a song they've learned, or everyone joins in with a well-known carol	✔	
10 minutes	Bible talk (Talk idea 1, page 20)		
5 minutes	Prizes and announcements		

Talk idea 1

Suitable for children's or family events

You will need to prepare the following visual aid as well as reading through the talk several times so that you are familiar with it.

Gear

▶ 9 sheets of card or wrapping paper, each labelled with one letter of the word CHRISTMAS

▶ 9 pictures (see page 84)—1 each of the following:
  Angels
  Census—a scroll
  Inn
  Sign saying "no room"
  Saviour—a nativity scene with Mary, Joseph and Jesus
  Shepherds
  Magi (wise men)
  Herod
  Treasure—the wise men's gifts

▶ A board / blank wall
▶ Blu-Tack reuseable adhesive or velcro

Stick the 9 pictures in a 3 x 3 grid:

Census scroll	Herod	"No room" sign
Inn	Saviour (nativity scene)	Treasure (the wise men's gifts)
Magi (wise men)	Angels	Shepherds

Then place the letter cards over the top:

C	H	R
I	S	T
M	A	S

Bible talk

What are you like at solving puzzles? Good? Great? Awwwwwwwwwesome? Well you've got a chance now to show me as we work through my very special Christmas puzzle. I'm going to choose a letter from the grid and all you have to do is work out what it could stand for in the true story of the very first Christmas. Ready?

Ok, so the first letter is... A. Any ideas? (Accept responses.)

A = ANGELS AND ANNOUNCEMENTS
(Remove letter "A" from the visual aid to reveal the picture underneath.)

About 2000 years ago in the town of Nazareth there was a young woman named Mary, who was told the most surprising thing. There she was, working at home, when all of a sudden an angel appeared in front her with an announcement: "Don't be afraid. God is pleased with you. He's chosen you to give birth to His Son, Jesus."

Mary thought it was impossible—how on earth could she have God's Son! But then the angel explained to her that the Holy Spirit, God's power, would come down and sort it because nothing is impossible with God.

Mary was pleased to be chosen but worried what Joseph, the man she was going to marry, would say when she told him her news.

Joseph didn't want to embarrass Mary in front of everyone so he decided to call off the wedding quietly. That was until an angel of the Lord came to him in a dream and said: "Joseph, the baby Mary will have is from God. Go ahead and marry her. Then after her baby is born, name Him Jesus because He will save His people from their sins."

Just to make matters worse, things got even more difficult with a "C"...

C = CENSUS
(Ask for suggestions for what the "C" might be, then remove letter "C" from the visual aid to reveal the picture underneath.)

The Roman emperor Augustus wanted to know how many people were in his empire and where they came from. So he commanded that a census (a count of everyone) must be taken throughout the Roman empire. So Joseph had to go to Bethlehem in Judea, where his family came from. He took Mary, the woman he was going to marry, with him.

It would have been a long and tiring journey—so when they arrived they looked for an "I"...

I = INN
(Ask for suggestions for what the "I" might be, then remove letter "I" from the visual aid to reveal the picture underneath.)

But Bethlehem was crammed and so there was no "R"___ for them.

R = ROOM (NO ROOM)
(Ask for suggestions for what the "R" might be, then remove letter "R" from the visual aid to reveal the picture underneath.)

It was when they arrived in Bethlehem that Mary gave birth to her child, a son. She wrapped Jesus snugly in strips of cloth and laid Him in a manger, since there was no room for them in the village inns. So, at last, after years of waiting, God's promised Rescuer had arrived. Our "S" had been born.

S = SAVIOUR
(Ask for suggestions for what the "S" might be, then remove letter "S" from the visual aid to reveal the picture underneath.)

You see, all of us disobey God and ignore Him. All of us tell lies, lose our temper, and don't treat God as He deserves. So all of us deserve to be punished by God—to be cut off from Him. But since the beginning of time, God had been promising that He would send His perfect Saviour to provide a way for us to be forgiven and to be friends with Him forever.

So how was God going to let people know He'd kept His promise and that His Son had arrived? Well, He began with some pretty unlikely people—some "S"...

S = SHEPHERDS
(Ask for suggestions for what the "S" might be, then remove letter "S" from the visual aid to reveal the picture underneath.)

At the same time, in some fields near Bethlehem, some shepherds were looking after their sheep. All at once a bright light appeared in the skies. They were terrified. It was an angel, sent by God, with the message not to be afraid, as they had some good news which was for everyone and would bring huge amounts of joy. The shepherds were told that down the hill in Bethlehem, that very night, God's Saviour had been born. Christ the Lord, God's chosen King, had arrived and was lying in an animal's feeding trough—lying in a manger.

The shepherds decided to go to Bethlehem to see what God had told them about. They dashed down the hill, probably tumbling as they went! But sure enough they found Mary and Joseph, and they saw Jesus lying in the hay. They were filled with joy and knelt down and worshipped baby Jesus.

They told Mary and Joseph how the angel had appeared in the sky and how Jesus would be the Saviour of the world.

As the shepherds were returning to their sheep, they were praising God and saying wonderful things about Him. God had really kept His promise of a Rescuer—someone who would rescue people from their sins. Everything the shepherds had seen and heard was just as the angel said.

And they weren't the only ones to see this. There were also some "M". (Or you could say "WM" if you think this would be clearer.)

M = MAGI (WISE MEN)
(Ask for suggestions for what the "M" might be, then remove letter "M" from the visual aid to reveal the picture underneath.)

Some time later, some wise men from eastern countries arrived in Jerusalem, asking questions. They had seen a new star shining in the sky and, having studied their scrolls, they knew that meant a new leader had been born.

They headed to the royal palace because they thought the new king would be there—but instead they found king "H"!

H = HEROD
(Ask for suggestions for what the "H" might be, then remove letter "H" from the visual aid to reveal the picture underneath.)

When Herod called the wise men in to see him, they asked to see the child who would be king of the Jews. Herod was worried and asked his advisors about it all. They told him that in the Old Testament history books it was written that God had promised that His king would be born in a little town called Bethlehem. So Herod told the wise men to go there. But Herod thought this new king may take away his throne, so he told the wise men to return to him afterwards and let him have directions to the boy. Herod pretended that he wanted to "worship" the child himself—but secretly, he wanted to have the child killed.

The star that the wise men had seen in the east had gone ahead of them, until it stopped over the place where the child was. The men got ready to give him "T".

T = TREASURE
(Ask for suggestions for what the "T" might be, then remove letter "T" from the visual aid to reveal the picture underneath.)

When the men went into the house, and saw Jesus with His mother, they knelt and worshipped. They gave him gifts of gold for a king, frankincense because He was God, and myrrh in preparation for His death.

When it was time to leave, the wise men went home another way, because God had warned them in a dream not to return to Herod. Herod was furious when he heard that the wise men had outwitted him. He sent soldiers to kill all boys under the age of two in the Bethlehem area. But Joseph had a dream where an angel told him to take Mary and Jesus to Egypt.

The soldiers did not find Jesus—He was safe in Egypt. And so He grew, and as He did, He lived a perfect life and did amazing things, which proved He was God. When Jesus was 33 years old, He died and rose again, taking the punishment we deserve for the wrong things we say, think and do. This was God's rescue plan to save us. Everyone who believes in Jesus the Rescuer, and trusts that His death paid the price for our sin, can be forgiven and become God's friend forever. This is what the angel meant when he told Joseph: "Name Him Jesus for He will save His people from their sins." This was God's rescue plan for us.

Talk idea 2
Suitable for children's events

You will need to collect the following things as well as reading the talk through several times so that you are familiar with it.

Gear

▶ Enough copies of the Eyewitness scripts (pages 22-23) for each person taking part
▶ Props and costumes if required

One person could play all four roles or you could have four different actors. The eyewitness accounts can be used in the following three ways:

1. All four parts in the same teaching slot, with a summary at the end.

2. Re-told by the characters, who are then "hot-seated" as the children ask them questions.

3. Re-told by the characters with the main leader adding a link after each one.

Details of these three options are given on pages 23-24.

Drama

Eyewitness accounts

(See page 23 for a choice of teaching slots to use after these eyewitness accounts. The person/people acting these roles may like to wear a simple Bible costume.)

Eyewitness 1—Mary

It was bizarre! There I was at home in Nazareth, when an angel came to visit me. ME! I didn't understand why. I was nothing special, just your average Nazareth teenager, although I did have a pretty special fiancé, Joseph—he was related to King David of old. Anyhow, this angel appears right before my eyes, says hello, calls me favoured and then tells me that God's with me.

I was pretty shaken—what was he talking about? Why had God sent me a messenger? I didn't need to wait long to find out. The angel, Gabriel, told me I had nothing to be afraid of but, all the same, God had chosen me to do a special job. God had planned for me to have a son called Jesus, who would be great and powerful, and known as the Son of the Most High. In fact, he went on to tell me that Jesus would be a King who ruled forever.

Well, you can imagine how shocked I was. How on earth was that even possible? I know a woman can't have a baby on her own—it needs a father. But when I asked Gabriel, he told me that the Holy Spirit would make the baby grow inside me. God would use His awesome power to provide a way for me to give birth to His perfect son.

I was also told that my cousin, who was way older than me, was pregnant, even though she'd never been able to have a baby. How cool is that! You see, nothing is impossible with God.

Well, by this stage I was finally getting my head round it and was ready to be God's servant. I agreed to it and told the angel I wanted it to all come true. At that, Gabriel went and left me to go break the news to Joseph... I'll let you find out for yourselves how he reacted, but put it this way—it wasn't looking good for the two of us for a few days!

Now I'd best be off. I have to go pack as the two of us—and this bump (rub tummy)—are about to head off to Bethlehem to register in the town where Joseph's ancestors come from. I hope we make it there in time...

Eyewitness 2—Joseph

So you know about Mary's news? Did she tell you I was all for calling off the wedding? That was until God showed me in a dream that it was all true, and I should go ahead and marry her. He made sure I knew that the child was from Him and was to be called Jesus, as the name means Saviour. That's what He was going to be—a Saviour. He was going to rescue people from their sins.

I couldn't believe it, and to be honest, I'm still finding it hard to believe that we are going to be raising God's Son, especially with us settled in among all the animals. It's hardly a place for a baby to be born, let alone a king—but it doesn't look like we have any choice. Bethlehem is packed out, what with the Roman census, so there's no room in any of the inns. Suppose it's better than nothing.

Oh… what's that? (Pauses with ear cupped.) **Sorry guys, I'd better head off. Mary's calling me. She says the baby's on its way. Jesus is about to be born. See ya!**

Eyewitness 3—Shepherds

'ey up! I'm one of the local shepherds. Just wanted to tell you about the most incredible night in my life! Me and my buddies were busy keeping an eye on our sheep as usual, when all of a sudden the sky lit up and an angel was stood among us! It was well scary.

The angel told us not to be scared as he had come with an amazing message from God. He told us that a brilliant event had taken place in Bethlehem which would bring total and utter joy to everyone, all over the world. The news was that God's promised Rescuer, His chosen King, had just been born and was lying in a manger in Bethlehem.

Then a load of other angels appeared and started a huge sing-song, giving God praise, as they sang: "Glory to God in the heavenly heights, and peace to anyone who pleases Him".

As they left, we all agreed that we had to get to Bethlehem as fast as we could and see for ourselves what God had revealed to us. We sprinted down the hill and found Mary, Joseph and Jesus, just as the angels said. It was fantastic! God has kept His promise by sending us His Saviour. We just had to tell everyone else the good news, I mean—how on earth could we keep that kind of info to ourselves?! Make sure you spread the word too…

Eyewitness 4—Wise men

Greetings! How are you, fine children? Now, I wonder, have you ever studied the sky at night? Do you know where "the Plough" ("the Big Dipper") is and "the Great Bear"? Do any of you own a telescope? Well if you do, then you would easily fit in with me and my fellow scholars. You see, we love looking at the stars and making notes on their positions, and it's because of that, we quickly spotted a brand new star, moving in a westward

direction not so long ago. We felt sure it was going to lead us to something special, someone special, a new king maybe, and so we followed it. We were keen to find the child and give him honour.

Now while we're not from these parts, everyone knows a king lives in a palace and so we went to the capital city of Jerusalem and sought out Herod. The next thing we knew, Herod had a whole crowd of advisors gathered around him. He demanded they tell him where God's chosen King was meant to be born.

They were quick to point out from their scrolls that God had always said His promised Rescuer would be born in Bethlehem. So Herod called us into a secret meeting and told us to go to Bethlehem, and make sure we found him. He seemed so keen to honour him and made us promise that we would return to him afterwards so he could also worship God's chosen King.

And so we set off, following the star we had seen in our eastern skies. It led us all the way to Bethlehem and hovered above a house there. We were convinced it was where God's chosen King, His promised Rescuer, would be and so we went on in because we had gifts to give.

Sure enough, there was Jesus with His mother, Mary, and so we knelt and worshipped Him. We gave Him gold since He is a king, frankincense since He is from God and myrrh for—well, myrhh for His death.

While we were in Bethlehem, God warned us in a dream not to report back to Herod because he meant to kill Jesus. So we worked out another route home to our country. We are sure God will keep Jesus safe, because He has a plan for Him.

Variation 1

All four eyewitness accounts in the same teaching slot, followed by this summary:

Isn't it incredible? God used lots of different ways to let these people and others know that His chosen King, His promised rescuer, His own precious Son had arrived. Why? Well because it was the best news in the world—EVER!

You see, Jesus came for one reason, and that was to bring people back to God, to make it so that people can once more be friends with God. The Bible says that we all do things that hurt God. We disobey Him and ignore Him, we say things wrong, think things wrong and do things wrong. The Bible calls this sin. We deserve to be punished by God.

But the Bible tells us that God loves us so much that He sent His only Son, Jesus, to be born as a baby, to live His life and then to die a horrible death on a cross—even though He had done nothing wrong. Jesus died in our place to take our punishment so we can be forgiven by God and become His friend forever.

Are you like Mary and Joseph? Do you believe that Jesus is our Saviour? Are you like the shepherds and the wise men? Will you celebrate Him? Will you thank Him for coming to die in your place? Do you want to live God's way, or are you like Herod and his men and choose to ignore Jesus and do your own thing?

Variation 2

Re-told by the characters, who are then "hot-seated" as the children ask them questions.

Hot seating is where people act out characters from a story and the children then ask them questions. The characters have to answer in as much detail as possible, from what we're told in the Bible.

Before the characters are interviewed, it is important to tell the children the answers will be based on the Bible. If a question is asked for which there is no information in the Bible, the character will need to explain that they cannot answer.

Afterwards, "hot-seat" a leader. Begin by asking them what they believe about the first Christmas and how Jesus' coming has made a difference in their life. Then allow children to ask related questions.

Variation 3

Re-told by the characters with the main leader adding a link after each one.

 After Mary's speech

Wow! Did you pick up on all that? God has chosen a young girl called Mary to give birth to His son. Did anyone pick out some of the phrases the angel used to tell us about Jesus? (Accept responses eg: great and powerful, an everlasting king.)

I wonder how Joseph will react? And more importantly, I wonder why God was sending His Son... we'll have to wait until later to find out.

 After Joseph's speech

So Joseph has stuck by Mary after all. Did anyone spot what Jesus' name means? (Saviour)

That answers why God was sending Jesus. He was sending Him to rescue us from the punishment we deserve. You see, all of us say, think and do wrong things, all of us put ourselves first instead

of living God's way, and the Bible teaches that we deserve to be punished for that. But Jesus came to take that punishment, to die in our place. He came to rescue us so we can be forgiven by God and become His friend forever.

 After the shepherd's speech

Did you see how excited the shepherd was by the news of Jesus' arrival? Are you like that? Do you understand that Jesus came to earth to die for you? Have you thanked Him for doing that? Have you said sorry for the times you've let Him down and ignored Him? Have you asked Him to forgive you and help you follow Him? If not, why not chat to one the leaders about it? And if you have, can you think of anyone you can tell the good news to this Christmas, like the shepherds did? After all, the angel said it was good news that would bring great joy for everyone.

 After the wise man's speech

I wonder if you're like the wise man. Do you know what? If you're not like the wise man, then really you're like Herod and his men who rejected Jesus. That means you are saying "no" to God and His rescue plan, and you won't be saved from God's punishment.

But if you are like the wise man, then you will want to look for Jesus and become His friend. You will ask Him to forgive you and start to live with Jesus as your King, doing what God wants you to do. You might not be able to give Him expensive gifts, but you can remember that Jesus was God's King and that He came to die. And you can show that He's important and precious to you when you make decisions, by thinking: What would please God?

IDEAS MENU

Four team challenges

These create team spirit and an enthusiastic environment. If you have divided the children into teams, get a representative up from each one.

Ice hockey team challenge

Gear
- ▶ A hockey stick
- ▶ A goal
- ▶ A puck
- ▶ If possible, hockey goalie gear

This is based on a penalty shoot-out competition. Have a leader in goal. Children to take it in turns to try and score. Points to be awarded for successful attempts.

Squirty snowballs team challenge

Gear
- ▶ A target board
- ▶ Squirty cream (ie: in an aerosol can)
- ▶ Plastic balls
- ▶ Tarpaulin

Children squirt squirty cream on to plastic balls and throw at a target board. Score points according to where they hit.

Bob-sleigh team challenge

Gear
- ▶ An office chair (or several if you want teams to compete at the same time)

Choose three volunteers from each team. Two children are to push the other child on the chair, a set distance and back. You could either time a team, or have them competing against each other if space allows.

Frozen fire team challenge

Gear
- ▶ Frozen peas
- ▶ Bowls—worth different points
- ▶ Masking tape for firing line

Have a variety of bowls for the children to fire peas into.

Each bowl is worth a different amount of points (eg: 3, 5, 10) depending on how close the bowl is. The children can fire the peas by flicking them from the palm of their hand. Or, if you're feeling brave, by putting a pea in their mouth and spitting it at the target! This is called "Frozen bogie spitting"!

Music spot

Choose from the following suggestions for the various song slots. You might also like to sing a well-known Christmas carol, especially if parents and the wider community have been invited.

The Bethlehem Bop (track 6) of Johnny Burns' *Praise Crazy* CD

Glory to God (track 22) of *The King, the snake and the promise* CD

The Saviour of the World (track 16) of the *Promises, promises* CD

He's Jesus (track 9) of the *Earth Movers* CD

The best thing (track 8) of Johnny Burns' *How cool is that!* CD

Jesus saves! (track 9) of Colin Buchanan's *Jesus rocks the world* CD

Any track from Colin Buchanan's *King of Christmas* CD

Memory verse

The Father has sent his Son to be the Saviour of the world.
1 John 4 v 14 (NIV)

Teach the whole verse to a beat, inviting children to slap their thighs and then clap their hands in order to keep the rhythm. After a few times through, you say the verse in the following way:

Leader: The Father has sent his Son to be the Saviour of the what?

Children: The Father has sent his Son to be the Saviour of the world!

Leader: The who has sent his Son to be the Saviour of the world?

Children: The Father has sent his Son to be the Saviour of the world!

Leader: The Father has sent his who to be the what of the world?

Children: The Father has sent his Son to be the Saviour of the world!

Christmas quiz ideas

Gear
- A cardboard Christmas tree
- Lots of card baubles/ornaments, with a variety of scores written on the back (see template on page 85)
- A range of questions based on the main teaching points and what has been covered in the session (see page 10 for more help in running quizzes)

Use the quiz to reinforce what has been taught in a fun way and to help teams score points. Make sure the questions are clear and pitched at all ages.

Christmas ornaments

Gear
- Paper plates, cut in half
- Polystyrene balls (about the size of a ping-pong ball and easy to find in most craft stores)
- Paper doily
- Scraps of fabric, foil, plastic jewels, tinsel / sparkly pipe cleaners
- PVA glue and sticky tape
- Pipe cleaners
- Wool or cotton wool balls
- Paints

Make a cone out of half a paper plate and stick together with sticky tape. Push a pipe cleaner through the polystyrene ball for a head, and twist a small knot at the top. Push the other end through the hole into the top of the cone. Twist the end inside the cone to make the head sit firmly on the body.

For an angel, paint the cone gold or silver and attach two wedge-shaped wings cut from a paper doily. Decorate the angel's gown with sparkly foil and plastic jewels. Finish by edging the bottom with a piece of sparkling tinsel. Draw the angel's face on the ball and glue a mop of hair using the wool, onto the scalp. Finally add a tiny circle of tinsel/sparkly pipe cleaner for a halo.

To make Mary, paint the cone blue and add a scrap of white fabric to her head. The same principle applies to making Joseph and the shepherds.

Christmas shortbread cookies

Gear
- 250g / 8oz butter
- 125g / 4oz caster sugar
- 350g /12oz plain flour
- Salt
- For decoration—glace icing, edible silver balls etc and ribbon

1. Mix the butter with the sugar until reasonably smooth.

2. Sift the flour and add a pinch of salt to the mixture.

3. Bring all the ingredients together into a ball and lightly knead to finish.

4. Roll out the cookie dough. Use Christmas cutters for shapes and make holes at the top with a skewer for hanging the cookies.

5. Bake the cookies on a greased baking tray in a pre-heated oven at 180°C (350°F, Gas mark 4) for about 10-15 minutes.

6. Once the cookies are cool, decorate with simple glace icing and edible silver balls, and attach ribbon.

Peppermint creams

Gear
- White from one large egg or two small eggs
- 225g / 8oz icing sugar
- Small amount of peppermint essence
- Food colouring (optional)
- Cutter
- Non-stick parchment / greaseproof paper

1. Beat the egg white in a bowl with a fork and sieve in 175g / 6oz of icing sugar.

2. Mix well with a wooden spoon and then sieve in more icing sugar, a little at a time, until you have made a stiff paste.

3. Shake a little icing sugar on the work surface and empty the paste onto this.

4. Add 3-4 drops of peppermint essence and gently knead until you have a smooth paste. Taste a small piece and if the flavour is not strong enough, add a few more drops of peppermint essence.

5. Sprinkle icing sugar over a rolling pin to prevent sticking, and roll the paste to a quarter of an inch (0.5cm) thick. Cut out individual peppermint creams with a cutter.

6. Cover a plate with non-stick parchment or greaseproof paper and place the peppermint creams on the paper.

7. Cover with a clean tea towel and leave overnight in a cool place (but not the fridge). Store in an airtight tin.

Jingle-bell bracelets

Gear
- Pipe cleaner, wrist or ankle size
- Bells
- Beads

1. To create a basic bracelet, just thread beads and bells on a wrist- or ankle-size pipe cleaner, then form it into a circle. Make a clasp by looping together the ends of the pipe cleaner.

2. For a fancier look, form a single pipe cleaner into a circle, thread on 4 or 5 bells, then coil additional pipe cleaners around the first, between each bell.

3. For a deluxe version, start with a bumpy pipe cleaner, threading 1 bell onto each "bump". Form a single pipe cleaner into a circle, then twist the bumpy pipe cleaner around it so that each bell faces outward.

Christmas banners

Gear

▶ Big letters (J – E – S- U- S)
▶ Tinsel
▶ Baubles/decorations
▶ Bells
▶ Wrapping paper
▶ Stickers
▶ PVA glue
▶ Bamboo canes
▶ Wallpaper or large fabric
▶ Staplers

1. Split children into groups. They are to cut out and decorate the letters with crayons—with images from the Christmas story.

2. They could also do additional names for Jesus in bubble writing (large open letters) and decorate eg: "Saviour", "Rescuer", "Son of God", "King" and cut out.

3. Spread out background fabric/paper banner. Position the letters and additional names of Jesus and then glue into place.

4. Make the background attractive by decorating with collage material. Attach banner to canes.

Paper bag reindeers

Gear

▶ Paper bags
▶ Red card / card stock
▶ Glue and scissors
▶ Markers or crayons
▶ Googly eyes

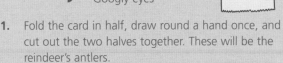

1. Fold the card in half, draw round a hand once, and cut out the two halves together. These will be the reindeer's antlers.

2. Fold the two top corners of a paper bag back to form the reindeer's head.

3. Glue, tape, or staple the handprints behind the reindeer's head.

4. Glue on googly eyes. Using the scraps of the red card, cut out and glue on a large, red nose. Glue them to the reindeer's face. Draw a mouth with a marker or crayons.

Wooden spoon Rudolph

Gear

▶ A wooden spoon
▶ Brown paint
▶ Brown foam
▶ Glitter (optional)
▶ Red pompom
▶ Googly eyes
▶ Black marker pen and glue

1. Paint the spoon and leave to dry.

2. Cut two antler shapes from foam.

3. Glue to the bowl of the spoon.

4. Add a little glue to the antlers and sprinkle glitter.

5. Glue on the pompom and eyes and draw a mouth.

Star decorations

Gear

▶ 6 lollipop sticks, if possible pre-coloured
▶ PVA glue
▶ Ribbon for hanging
▶ Decorations—metallic paint, sequins, jewels, glitter, pens etc

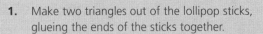

1. Make two triangles out of the lollipop sticks, glueing the ends of the sticks together.

2. Thread a loop of ribbon onto one of the triangles so the star can be hung.

3. When dry, position one triangle on top of the other and glue at the places where the two triangles join.

4. When dry, decorate your star!

Christmas cards

Gear

▶ A pile of blank cards
▶ Stickers and stamps
▶ PVA glue to hand.

Some ideas:

1. A stuck-on Christmas tree shape, decorated with silver foil baubles and dots of tinsel for a 3-D effect.

2. A snowman shape against black card. Paste his body with glue and balls of fluffy cotton wool. Add a bright card hat and fabric scarf.

3. Cover a card with intricate miniature snowflakes.

Cut these out by folding white paper circles into wedges and making random cuts. When you unfold the wedge, you have a magical snowflake.

4. Make a simple Christmas collage card created from last year's Christmas cards. Use images and letters to create a striking new picture and greeting.

Prayer

Remind the children that at Christmas time we remember that God sent His Son to earth, that Jesus is God with us. Ask children to stretch out one arm, with the palm facing sideways. As you say the words: "Jesus is God with us", the children are to bend one finger at a time (ie: "Jesus" = little finger; "is" = ring finger; "God" = middle finger; "with" = index finger) until you get to "us" when they raise their thumb up. Explain the fact that Jesus is God with us is worth celebrating lots—it's worth thumbs up and a lot more! Ask the children to brainstorm why (eg: we're never alone, we know we can be forgiven…).

Say "Jesus is God with us" once more, and while the children have their thumbs up, say a prayer with them.

Thank You Lord God for sending Jesus into this world. Thank You that He came to be our Rescuer. Thank You that we can be forgiven and friends with You, because of Jesus' death. Thank You that You are always with us and never let us down. Amen

Small groups

Options A and B both include time for the children to be split into small groups where they can think about the teaching they have heard. We suggest that these groups meet for 15 minutes, just after the main teaching slot.

Pages 33-35 include copies of fun sheets to use in these groups. The sheets have been designed for three age groups: 4-7s (Reception to Year 2)—page 33, 7-9s (Years 3-4)—page 34, 9-11s (Years 5-6)—page 35. With the older groups, you may also choose to have Bibles available so that they can read for themselves some of the Bible story they have heard. If you don't have sufficient Bibles available, you can copy the relevant text from www.biblegateway.com to print your own sheets.

On pages 31-32 there are notes to help the leaders of the small groups. Please give copies of these to each small-group leader in advance, so that they can prepare thoroughly. This is particularly important if the small groups are being led by an inexperienced leader or helper (which may be the case if you have a small team and a large number of children).

Christmas DVDs

Choose from the following DVDs:

Christmas Storykeepers (ISBN VD667)

Punchinello and the most marvellous gift (ISBN VD711)

It's a Boy (ISBN FIERDVD20)

Nativity the DVD (ISBN VD699)

Snowball fight

Gear
▶ Balls wrapped in tissue paper

Divide the room into four. Have a few large soft balls covered in tissue paper. Teams are to try and keep them out of their quadrant. The team that has the most balls in their area each time the whistle blows loses a life.

Snowmen and some!

Gear
▶ Toilet paper rolls
▶ Scarves
▶ Hats
▶ Carrots
▶ Red and green fabric
▶ Lights
▶ Wellies / rubber boots
▶ Cotton wool balls
▶ Cushions

Split the children into teams. Ask them to make the best looking snowman using toilet roll, a scarf, hat and carrot; a best looking Santa with red fabric, cushions, cotton wool and wellies; and a Christmas tree with fabric, lights and decorations. Give them a set amount of time and then judge.

Rapidough

Gear
▶ List of 15 Christmas items eg: star, angel, wise man, manger...
▶ Playdough

Split children into teams. One volunteer from each team is shown a word which they must sculpt in the playdough. How many words will the group manage to guess within two minutes?

Nativity signature bingo
(juniors/adults only)

Gear
▶ Pens
▶ Bingo sheets (see page 87)

Hand out the sheets and pens. Children are to race

around collecting signatures of others who fit the criteria on the grid (no more than 2-3 of the same person). The first person to finish is the winner.

Nativity scavenger hunt

Gear
▶ List of items to bring (see below).

Divide the children into teams. Each team is to designate a runner. Ask the runner to bring something from the list to you. The first one there scores a point. Continue until the list is finished.

1. Something soft to wrap the baby in

2. Sheep's wool

3. Something gold

4. Money to pay the innkeeper (extra points to the most)

5. Something suitable for the baby to sleep in

6. Something sweet-smelling like frankincense

7. A book for the census to be recorded in

8. Something shiny and something white to represent the angel

9. A piece of wood for Joseph the carpenter to work on

10. 3 team members acting—one as a donkey, another as a sheep and the third as a camel

11. A picture of royalty

12. Something to cover a head with

Christmas nativity

(This game is a variation on "Shipwreck".) When you call out a particular word, the children have to run to that place or do that action. Eliminate those who are last. Name the four walls: Nazareth, Bethlehem, Jerusalem and the East. (When you call out one of them, the children need to run to that wall.) Other commands are: "Shepherds arriving"—everyone on all fours going "baaaa"; "Wise men coming"—in twos, piggy back (riding on a camel!); "Baby's sleeping"—fingers to lips going "Shhhhhhhh"; "Angels arriving"—lie on floor and move arms up and down like angel wings.

Christmas dinner

Children stay in circles with one standing in the middle. All given the name of a kind of Christmas food. Eg: Christmas pudding / Yule log / Turkey / Brussel sprout (choose food the children will be familiar with). When their food

name is called, they must change seats with another child. The standing person has to try and sit down. Whoever is left standing is on next. When "Christmas dinner" is called, everyone must change seats.

Chocolate shepherd game

Gear
▶ Dressing gowns
▶ Tea-towels
▶ Chocolate
▶ Dice
▶ Tray
▶ Knife and fork

Put the bar of chocolate on the plate with the knives and forks nearby and sit the children around it in a circle. Put a dressing gown and tea towel in the middle of the circle. Give one child the dice.

Children take it in turns to roll the dice on the floor in front of them, passing it around the circle to their left. If a child rolls a six, they have to go into the middle of the circle, put on the dressing gown and tea-towel, and start to unwrap, then eat, the bar of chocolate—but only using the knife and fork. That child keeps going until another child rolls a six, at which point they must co-operate in handing over the clothes so that the next child gets a turn.

Christmas corners

Gear
▶ Labels for the room corners eg: sheep, king, star, baby
▶ Christmas music

Label four corners of the room. Give actions for each one. Children dance around to Christmas music and then, when it stops, they run to a corner and do that action. The person in the middle chooses a corner / card with corner on. Whoever is in that corner is out.

Christmas card chaos

Gear
▶ Old Christmas cards
▶ Box

Set up a "course" by placing a large box or bin on the floor and marking a place to stand some feet away from it (how far depends on the age of the children). Each child takes turns tossing a stack of cards (like a frisbee) into the box. Count up and the child with the most cards in the box wins.

Pass the Christmas ornament

Games

Gear
- One straw for each child
- Ornaments cut out of tissue paper (tree, bell, star, etc)

Divide the children into two teams and line up each team. Pass the ornaments down the line, child to child, by inhaling and exhaling on the straw to hang onto or release the ornament. No hands! The first team to pass the ornaments up and down the line wins!

Pin the nose on Rudolph

Games

Gear
- Picture of a noseless Rudolf
- Scarf / airline sleep mask
- Red nose
- Blu-Tack reuseable adhesive

This is basically "pin the tail on the donkey". Stick a picture of Rudolf on the wall, blindfold one child at a time, spin them around and see if they can pin a red nose in the right place. The nearest wins a prize/points.

Rudolph relay race

Games

Gear
- Circles cut out of red tissue paper
- Vaseline

Split into teams. Using Vaseline have the first child in each queue put a blob of Vaseline on their nose and stick a red circle on. They have to run to the finish, then the next person goes. If the nose falls off, the runner must go back to the bowl and add more Vaseline to reapply their nose.

Stocking filler

Games

Gear
- Christmas stocking for each team
- Spoon for each team
- Bowl for each team
- Wrapped sweets

Divide the children into teams and line the teams up at one end of the room. At the other end, hang a Christmas stocking for each team. Place a bowl of sweets and a spoon in front of each team. The first child in each team takes a sweet from the bowl with the spoon. They carry the sweet on the spoon to the stocking, drop it in, and race back to the next person. The second child in line then takes the spoon and so on.

Either play that the first team to fill the stocking are the winners, or play for a set amount of time and the team with the most sweets in their stocking in that time wins.

Superstars wall quiz

Games

As children arrive, have numbered pictures of superstars around the room. The children have a numbered piece of paper and pencil, and walk around, jotting the names down.

Who's Santa?

Games

(This game is based on "wink murder".) One child is selected to be Rudolph and leaves the room while Santa is selected. One person from the circle is elected to be Santa, and then Rudolph is called back to stand in the circle. Once Rudolph returns, Santa can start winking at people in the circle. Anyone who sees that they have been winked at lets out a loud "HO! HO! HO!—Merry Christmas!" Rudolph has to guess who Santa is.

Starbash

Games

Gear
- Black bin liners / garbage bags
- Balloons

Split children into two teams and have them sit down facing each other with a small gap in the centre. Insist that the children stay seated for the whole game. To score a goal, the children have to use their hands to hit the balloon bag (a bin liner filled with 5 balloons) over the heads of the opposing team so that it lands in the opposition territory.

Ski-ing plank race

Games

Gear
- Planks—with ropes attached at both ends for the children standing at the front and back to hold.
- Cones

Team members must stand one behind another astride two planks (as if on giant skis). They must work as a team to race across a set distance.

Ice-cube race

Games

Gear
- Ice cubes
- Bowls
- Towels

Line up each team. They will pass ice cubes down their backs. The ice cube is passed out at the bottom of one person's shirt into the top of the next shirt. If it falls, start over. Points for the number of ice cubes passed.

Leading a small group—notes for leaders

- Sit the children in a circle.

Ice-breaker:

- Start by introducing yourself and maybe say your favourite chocolate bar / colour / food.

- Ask children to do the same.

- Ask them what they have liked best so far today… and maybe share with them your favourite bit too!

Fun sheet:

- Explain that we are going to be thinking about the story we just heard.

- Give out a sheet each and pencil or felt-tip pen. Ask them to write their name on the sheet.

- Work through the questions one at a time, using the attached notes to help you. Encourage the children to talk about each question together, rather than racing ahead.

- Encourage them to complete the colouring and puzzle on the back at home. If they are coming to another event at church, or are a member of a weekly church club, then ask them to bring the sheet back and show you.

Memory verse:

If you have extra time at the end of the sheet, remind the children of the memory verse: "The Father has sent his Son to be the Saviour of the world." 1 John 4 v 14

There are a number of ways that you can practise the memory verse:

- Start small, build up
- Use actions or have pictures/symbols instead of, or as well as, words
- Jigsaw puzzle
- Word-cards / balloons (could mix order)—gradually take away or pop balloons
- A code
- March it / clap it
- Rap or song

Notes on questions for 4-7s (Reception to Year 2)

1. What gave Mary her special message?

Question 1 is pretty straightforward. Don't forget to sell it to them eg: "Who here is clever enough to remember from the story…?"

2. Who really gave Jesus His name?

Unpack why it was God who should choose the name—Jesus was His Son.

3. Jesus means "God saves". Why is that a good name for Him? Draw your answer if you like.

Use question 3 to check your children understand the gospel eg: Jesus came to save us from the punishment we deserve for the wrong things we do and for not treating Him as King. And He came to save us to make us His friends forever.

4. Draw how the shepherds felt after they saw the angel and after they saw Jesus. Also draw a friend you could tell about Jesus—copying the shepherds' example.

On question 4, maybe get them to show you the shepherds' expressions first by acting them out. After they've drawn all three, ask them who their friend is and one way they could tell them about Jesus eg: invite them along to club.

5. Think about the wise men. How can we show we love Jesus and treat Him as the King?

We can give our obedience (hearts)—do what He says; our time—spend time learning about Him, talking to Him, doing things that help others and please Him (have practical examples ready). We can give thanks—celebrate how amazing God is. We can even give our money!

Notes on questions for 7-9s (Years 3 and 4)

1.   Why was "Jesus" such a great name for Him?

Use question 1 to check your children understand the gospel eg: Jesus means "God saves". It's a great name as Jesus came to save us from the punishment we deserve for the wrong things we do and for not treating Him as King. And He came to save us to make us His friends forever.

2.   How did the angel's message for the shepherds back this up?

Before asking question 2, check that the children remember the angel's message. Then in answering the question, help them see that the angel actually had the best news in the whole world, EVER! For hundreds of years, people had been waiting for God's Rescuer and now He had arrived—a way to be forgiven and be friends with God had come.

3.   The shepherds told lots of people about Jesus. Write down the name of a friend you can tell about Jesus.

When you're moving on to question 3, ask the children how we can be like the shepherds eg: we should listen to God (in the Bible). We can try to find out more about Jesus.

We can tell our friends about the good news that they can be friends of God. After asking the children to write down their friend's name, challenge them to think how they can do that. Give some practical suggestions.

4.   What did the wise men's gifts show about Jesus?

On question 4 make sure the children know the gifts showed different things about Jesus. The gold showed that Jesus was a King; the frankincense, because it was used in temples/prayer, showed Jesus was God; and the myrrh showed He would die a special death. You see, all along, God had a plan to rescue us!

5.   How can we show we love Jesus and treat Him as King?

We can give our obedience (hearts)—do what He says; our time—spend time learning about Him, talking to Him, doing things that help others and please Him (have practical examples ready). We can give thanks—celebrate how amazing God is. We can even give our money!

Notes on questions for 9-11s (Years 5 and 6)

1.   How do we know Jesus was 100% God and 100% man?

Work through with the children how Jesus was God in "skin". We know this through the message the angel passed on, as well as through the life Jesus went on to live. Help unpack why this is important. Jesus was 100% God, so 100% perfect and powerful and therefore able to take the punishment we deserve. And He's 100% man, so He would still be tempted as we are, go through tough times like we do, and be able to be our substitute.

2.   Put the angel's message to the shepherds into your own words.

Things to draw out here are: the fact that it was a message that would affect everyone; for hundreds of years, people had been waiting for God's Rescuer and now He had arrived; God's chosen King had come and now a way to be forgiven and be friends with God had come. *The Message* puts it this way: "Don't be afraid. I'm here to announce a great and joyful event that is meant for everybody, worldwide: A Saviour has just been born in David's town, a Saviour who is Messiah and Master."

3.   The shepherds told lots of people about Jesus. Do you think it's still a message worth sharing? Why / why not?

Question 3 will give you insight into where the children are at. Be sure to take the opportunity to explain why you think it is a message worth sharing. If appropriate, share a little of your own testimony.

4.   What did the wise men's gifts show about Jesus?

On question 4 make sure the children know the gifts showed different things about Jesus. The gold showed that Jesus was a King; the frankincense, because it was used in temples/prayer, showed Jesus was God; and the myrrh showed He would die a special death. You see, all along, God had a plan to rescue us!

5.   Who are you more like—the wise men or Herod? Why?

Again question 5 is an "insight-provider". The idea is that maybe we're like Herod, who knew who Jesus was but wanted to get rid of Him. He wanted to live his own way and not allow Jesus to be King. Or we can be like the wise men, who worshipped Jesus and gave Him gifts. We can give our obedience (hearts)—do what He says; our time—spend time learning about Him, talking to Him, doing things that help others and please Him (have practical examples ready). We can give thanks—celebrate how amazing God is. We can even give our money!

ONE DAY WONDERS

CHRISTMAS CRACKERS

The Father has sent his Son to be the Saviour of the world.

1 John 4 v 14

1. What gave Mary her special message?

2. Who really gave Jesus His name?

3. Jesus means "God saves". Why is that a good name for Him? Draw your answer if you like.

4. Draw how the shepherds felt after they saw the angel and after they saw Jesus. Also draw a friend you could tell about Jesus. (That's how you can copy the shepherds.)

5. Think about the wise men. How can we show we love Jesus and treat Him as the King?

CHRISTMAS CRACKERS

Joseph saw an angel in a dream. The angel told him about Mary and Jesus.

Colour in the picture.

Wise men, called Magi, came from the east to visit the new King. They had special gifts for King Jesus.

Help the wise men find their way to Jesus.

CHRISTMAS CRACKERS

The Father has sent his Son to be the Saviour of the world.

1 John 4 v 14

1. Why was "Jesus" such a great name for Him?

2. How did the angel's message for the shepherds back this up?

3. The shepherds told lots of people about Jesus. Write down the name of a friend you can tell about Jesus.

4. What did the wise men's gifts show about Jesus?

5. How can we show we love Jesus and treat Him as King?

CHRISTMAS CRACKERS

"Do not be **afraid**. I **bring** you **good news** of **great joy** that **will** be for **all** the **people**. **Today** in the **town** of **David** a **Saviour** has been **born** to you; he is **Christ** the **Lord**."

Luke 2 v 10-11

"**Glory** to **God** in the **highest**, and on **earth** **peace** to **men** on whom his **favour** rests."

Luke 2 v 14

H	S	P	O	M	S	B	L	E	B	G
I	A	E	N	G	A	A	R	O	O	O
G	L	O	R	Y	V	F	E	I	R	O
H	L	P	S	S	I	R	M	E	N	D
E	E	L	P	J	O	A	R	N	E	G
S	G	E	E	O	U	I	U	T	W	T
T	O	D	A	Y	R	D	O	W	S	O
B	D	Y	C	R	D	A	V	I	D	W
G	G	R	E	A	T	O	A	L	D	N
C	H	R	I	S	T	H	F	L	L	A

Find the **bold** words in the wordsearch. Some are diagonal - or backwards!

Now copy the left-over letters (in order) to find out who said these words.

_ _ _ _   _ _ _ _ _ _ _ _ _ _

ONE DAY WONDERS

CHRISTMAS CRACKERS

The Father has sent his Son to be the Saviour of the world.
1 John 4 v 14

1. How do we know that Jesus was 100% God and 100% man?

2. Put the angel's message to the shepherds into your own words.

3. The shepherds told lots of people about Jesus. Do you think it's still a message worth sharing? Why / why not?

4. What did the wise men's gifts show about Jesus?

5. Who are you more like—the wise men or Herod? Why?

CHRISTMAS CRACKERS

An angel told Joseph that Mary was going to have a son, who was to be called Jesus.

Crack the star code to see what the name **Jesus** means.

 _ _ _   _ _ _ _ _ _

It tells us **who** Jesus is – He is **G** _ _

It tells us **what** Jesus does – He **S** _ _ _ _ _

Jesus was given another great name as well – the name Immanuel.

What does **Immanual** mean?

 _ _ _   _ _ _ _ _   _ _ _

These brilliant names tell us loads about God. You could read about them for yourself in Matthew 1 v 18-25.

It's a Kind of Magi

Scene 1: News office

Announcer:
When Jesus was born, in days long past,
There was no TV to spread the news fast,
But just for a while, imagine there had been,
How do you think they'd have reported the scene?
Well, let's go back and find out today,
Through our "It's a kind of Magi" Christmas play!

Newsreader 1: *(Shaking their newspaper)*
News! News! Get your evening news!
Shock tax tactics! Will the Romans lose?
Emperor orders census, all must go
Back to the town of their family's abode!

Editor:
Now listen up guys, a big story's breaking.
If we get to it first, it could be our making.
Let's cover the census from a different view,
A family-interest angle with a twist or two.

Journalist 1:
What you on about boss? That seems rather flat.
A lady and a baby? Where's the fun in that?

Editor:
Ah, you've got it wrong—it's special in every sense.
With stars and royalty involved, it's simply immense.
In fact it's even better, as God's played a part
In sending an angel to launch His mission start.

Journalist 2:
I've heard that too sir, God's chosen Mary
To have His Son, and even though it's scary,
To call Him Jesus, for a Saviour He will be,
And though she didn't get it all, Mary agreed.

Journalist 1:
But that's crazy sir, why would Joseph stay?
Surely he'd have ditched her and run away?

Journalist 2:
He would have done but he saw an angel too,
Who told him it was God's plan, good and true.
He knew he had to marry, and at the child's birth,
Call Him Jesus for He'll be the "Saviour" of the earth.

Editor:
It's just like Isaiah said, all those years ago.
It's finally happened, so off you go!
The waiting has seemed like insanity,
But this dawn will affect all eternity!

Journalist 1 and 2 leave to the right, editor to the left.

Scene 2: Bethlehem

Newsreader 2: *(News headlines music)*
Good evening to all viewers, wherever you are,
For the census you may have had to travel far.
One very crowded place is Bethlehem town,
Our correspondent's there to see who's around.
Good evening, _____ and _____.
How are things tonight in Bethlehem?

Journalist 1:
Good evening, from a very crowded town.
As you can see, there are people all around.
(Wave arm around behind.)

Journalist 3:
Yes that's right, they're simply filling the streets.
The innkeepers seem to be run off their feet.
Let's chat to one and see how it's been.
Excuse me sir, how full is your inn?

Innkeeper:
Full? FULL? Full to the brim, no room left at all.
In fact, I've even lent my stable to one couple.
She's just had her baby among the hay,
And called Him Jesus, so her husband says.

Journalist 3: *(Very excitedly)*
Did you hear that? The Rescuer has come.
We'll try to get in and find out about the son.
We also need to find somewhere to nap
So I'll hand back to the studio for the next lap.

Newsreader 1:
Well thank you very much for that news,
We'll return later to hear other views.
But for now we'll cross over to the grassy banks,
To find out how things are in the shepherds' ranks.

Journalist 2:
Hello, here we are looking down on the town.
It's all very quiet, only the sheep around.

Journalist 4:
And of course the shepherds, how are you?
How are you coping with those coming through?

Shepherd 1:
To be honest, chum, it's making us jumpy!

ONE DAY WONDERS

Journalist 4:
That sounds like a joke! Woolly Jumper—jumpy!

Shepherd 2:
We're all feeling it, like something's about to pass.
Can't settle down at night, on the grass.

Shepherd 3:
It's like a bell that rings inside our mind.
It's challenging the doors of time.

Shepherd 4: *(Angel enters)*
Yikes—look at that! There's an angel just come!
Why's it here? Shall we go on the run?

Gabriel:
Don't be afraid, I've got some good news
For all the world, not just for Jews.
God's Son's been born in Bethlehem tonight.
He's on a rescue mission to put things right.
He's the shaft of light that shows the way,
The immortal God-man that'll win the day.
You'll find him wrapped in cloth, lying in the straw.
Hurry down to see Him, go and adore!

Other angels:
Glory to God in Heaven, who reigns over all.
Peace on earth to God's people, one and all.
(Angels sit down)

Shepherd 1: *(Stands up and pulls at others)*
Come on then, why hang around?
You all heard that angel sound.

Journalist 4: *(To the audience)*
This is sensational! How amazing!
Angels singing while the sheep are grazing!
Let's follow them down and see this boy
Who brings hope to us all and such joy.

Newsreader 2:
Let's do exactly that, faithful viewers.
And for all you chariot-racing pursuers,
The race will be shown, as soon as we are able,
But for now, what's the latest from the stable?

Journalist 1:
Well I'm standing outside the small, smelly stable.
Shepherds are packed in, as many as are able.
They are talking to Mary about what they just saw,
And seem to be filled with wonder and awe.

Journalist 4:
Let's speak to them now as they get ready to leave.
(Turn to the shepherds)
How do you feel? What do you believe?

Shepherd 2:
Excited and glad, God chose to tell us.

Shepherd 3:
And being the first is a real plus.

Shepherd 4:
We've got to tell others, right here, right now.

Journalist 4:
So it's back to you _____ in the studio.

Scene 3: Some time later...

Newsreader 1:
Good evening viewers and to all of you—welcome.
Today we're following up on the news of God's Son.
We're going to find out how things are with his folks,
But first to the palace, where some news has just broke!

Journalist 5:
Good evening from Herod's mighty abode.
A few men have arrived from the eastern road.
They asked to see the new king as soon as they came,
And that's why Herod's in a mood, they're to blame.

Journalist 6:
Yes that's right, they're a kind of Magi from afar.
They were studying the sky and spotted a new star.
They knew from their books that it meant God's King,
And so they have come to see and worship Him.

Journalist 5:
Let's chat to them and find out what Herod said.
Hey guys, over here, give us info for our spread.
Tell us what went on and why you're leaving here.
Herod seems angry and you—full of fear.

Wise man 1:
Well, when we spoke to Herod, he went pale,
And then all his advisors he did hail.
They checked out their scrolls and said to him
What Micah had said about the birth of God's King.

Wise man 2:

They told Herod He'd be born in Bethlehem,
A town just south-west of Jerusalem.
God's King had been sent to set people free,
Which left Herod as worried as he could be.

Wise man 3:

Herod seemed to us such a sneaky man.
He came back and told us he had a plan.
He told us to find this Saviour, and tell him when we do,
For he'd really like to go and see; he wants to worship too!

Wise man 4:

We're not convinced by him, but we are by God,
So we've got our gifts and to the town we'll plod.
Come along with us, follow the star as well.
Who knows what you'll see and stories you will tell.

Journalist 6:

So Herod's got a problem, he's forgotten he's just a man,
No one in the world can ever stop God's plan!
If this child's the Saviour, let us each and every one
Seek Him ourselves, as our Magi have done.

Journalist 1:

Thanks _____. We're actually outside their house,
But you'll notice it's as quiet as a mouse.
The reason is quite simple, they've all gone.
The Magi have fled and the family too at dawn.

Journalist 3:

This was after they gave gifts for the boy.
He's the world's Rescuer, the one who'll bring us joy:
Frankincense, a gift for God, and gold for a King,
They also brought Him myrrh, for His death and suffering.

Journalist 5:

Then in a dream they were warned to flee from the place,
To go a different way, not return to the palace,
The news had filled Herod with anger and dread.
He planned to come and strike this God-sent infant dead!

Journalist 6:

An angel also spoke to Joe in a dream,
And warned him of King Herod's evil scheme,
And so they left from here, before it was light,
And headed towards Egypt in the dead of night.

Announcer:

Well that's not the beginning nor is it the end.
So what's it all about? Why was Jesus sent?
What were the gifts about? Was there something more?
Well let's stop to think on this—and truths explore.

Narrator 1:

Long, long ago when the world by God was made,
We were made to be His friends and to follow His way.
But people choose to disobey and ignore Him,
And so there's a problem with a thing called sin.

Narrator 2:

God hates sin and, though it's sad,
We're barred from Heaven 'cos we're bad.
But there's great news that'll warm your heart:
God offers to us all a brand-new start.

Narrator 1:

For in love, God sent His only Son,
Who died for sin and victory won.
"King of the Jews" the sign did say…

Wise man 1:

Gold, a gift for a king we gave that day.

Narrator 2:

He paid the price as He hung up high…

Wise man 2:

Myrrh, a gift for the one who must die.

Narrator 2:

No barrier now, if we will pray,
Admit our sin and sorry say.
We can be forgiven through what He's done…

Wise man 3:

Frankincense, a gift for God's Son.

Narrator 1:

He wants to clean your heart from sin…

Wise man 4:

And hear you say to Him: "Come in!"

Announcer:

So it's not a kind of magi or magic,
And it's certainly not a myth nor tragic.
It's all about God's amazing love for us;
So right now, to Him will you turn and trust?

Combining parts: *This drama script has 24 speaking parts. However, many of the parts can be merged to reduce the number of children needed. Eg: have 1 newsreader, 3 journalists, 2 shepherds, 2 wise men. The editor can also be narrator 1.*

ONE DAY WONDERS

② THE TOTALLY EGGSCELLENT EASTER EGGSPERIENCE

LUKE 19 v 28-48: 22 v 1 – 24 v 12

Aim

To help the children (and their families if it's a family event) to:

▶ know that Jesus is the only one worthy to take our punishment for our sin.
▶ understand that Jesus died and rose again, showing that He is God and salvation is available for all.

Memory verse

For Christ died for sins once for all, the righteous for the unrighteous, to bring you to God. 1 Peter 3 v 18a (NIV)

Notes for leaders

 Read **Luke 19 v 28-48; 22 v 1 – 24 v 12.**

The major theme in Luke's Gospel is that "salvation is available for all". As you work through the events of the first Easter week, that message becomes more and more apparent.

While the main emphasis is on Jesus' death and resurrection, we start with Jesus' triumphal entry into Jerusalem (**Luke 19 v 28-48**). As the crowds eagerly wait for their Messiah to overthrow the Romans and free Israel, Jesus fulfils **Zechariah 9 v 9** by riding in on a colt. It is a clear sign of His kingship and intention to save, as well as a reminder that He knows everything, and that His death was according to plan (**Luke 19 v 28-35**).

This public demonstration by Jesus sees the opposition against Him grow, and through the following chapters the Pharisees and other religious leaders try to catch Him out. Eventually they have an opportunity to arrest and kill Him—on the night of the Passover.

As Jesus talks to His disciples (**Luke 22 v 7-38**), then His Father (**v 39-46**) and lastly those who've arrested Him (**v 47-53**), it's clear why He has come—to bring salvation to all through His death. God's own dear Son is the one who gave Himself to pay for our sin (**John 10 v 18**).

After His arrest, Jesus is accused falsely and stays faithful to the truth—while Peter is accused truly and lies (**Luke 22 v 54 – 23 v 12**). The challenge for us is to consider how we respond to times of suffering and temptation and to think how can we faithfully teach others to stand firm, whatever the cost.

Pontius Pilate takes the coward's way out. He gives the crowds a choice: between a murderer or the King of the Jews. Incited by the religious leaders, the crowd demand that Barabbas, the murderer, be released. And so Jesus is Barabbas' substitute (**Luke 23 v 13-25**), as well as ours.

The thief on the cross is a great example of how to receive salvation. He'd committed a crime worthy of death, he wasn't worthy of being right with God, yet he sees that Jesus is innocent (v 41) and God's chosen King (v 42). He understands that Jesus is the only way to heaven and he believes Jesus has the power to provide a way there for him. Let's pray those we're working with would see their need and ask to be allowed into God's kingdom too.

Chapter 24 shows clearly that death could not defeat Jesus, and that we have a glorious risen King. In the early verses (v 1-12) we have an eyewitness account from the women that the stone is moved away (v 2),that the tomb is empty (v 3), that they saw an angel (v 4) and that Jesus is alive and can be met (v 6). Peter and John also witness the empty tomb, and the following verses offer us more and more evidence for our hope in the gospel.

Pray

Leader's prayer

Father God, thank You so much that Jesus died in our place, taking the punishment we deserve, so that we may be saved. Thank You for the hope we have in the gospel because of His resurrection. Please help us unashamedly to teach the gospel and please bring others into Your kingdom, as you did with the thief on the cross. Amen.

Programme Options

Easter, like Christmas, presents churches with a unique gospel opportunity, as people are often more willing to come along to church-based special events.

You could use the programmes below as:
- a part of your church-wide Easter outreach programme.
- an end-of-term special for your regular children's groups.
- an event a few weeks before Easter, as a pre-runner for an Easter Holiday Club.

See the **"Aims"** section on page 6 to help you decide who you want to reach out to.

Once you have decided upon your target audience, choose an outline from the three options below. Then select games, crafts, challenges etc (see **Ideas Menu**, pages 49-54) and delegate accordingly.

The tables on the next three pages give you further details about each of the three suggested options for an Easter event. Space is included to add the name of the team member responsible for each activity. You may find it helpful to give copies of this table to each member of your team. You can photocopy this page or download a copy for free from
www.thegoodbook.co.uk/onedaywonders
(see page 3 for more details about downloads).

Option A: Two-hour children's event

15 min	Registration and opening games (begins 10 min before start time)
25 min	Together Time 1—songs, team challenges, memory verse, quiz
25 min	Themed crafts (with drinks break)
25 min	Together Time 2—songs, team challenges, Bible story, prayer, quiz
15 min	Small groups
25 min	Themed games

Option B: Four hour children's event
with parents invited to come and watch performance at end

15 min	Registration and opening games (begins 10 min before start time)
25 min	Together Time 1—songs, team challenges, "Eyewitness 1", prayer
25 min	Themed crafts (with drinks break)
25 min	Together Time 2—songs, team challenges, "Eyewitness 2", quiz (1)
25 min	Themed games
25 min	Together Time 3—songs, team challenges, "Eyewitness 3", memory verse
40 min	Younger children watch Easter DVD, older children rehearse play and some make props / Easter treats
25 min	Together Time 4—songs, team challenges, "Eyewitness 4", quiz (2)
20 min	Small groups
25 min	Food, final set-up and prizes
30 min	Performance—parents come and watch songs, verse and play

Option C: One-and-a-half-hour family fun event

15 min	Various "egg games" as families arrive
50 min	Games: Teams of family groups to move around a number of side-stalls, competing in each. Rotate round every three minutes.
15 min	Festive refreshments
10 min	Talk
5 mins	Prizes

Option A: Two-hour children's event

2 *Easter Fun*

Gear

- Name labels and pens
- Registration forms
- Colouring sheets and pencils
- Materials for your choice of games, challenges and crafts
- Visual aids for the Bible story
- Memory-verse props

- Music and words for songs
- Quiz questions and scoreboard
- Small-group sheets and pencils for each child
- Prizes
- Refreshments
- Publicity for Easter services or events

Time	Activity	✔	Leader
	Tick when materials are ready for each activity		
Before event	Preparation eg: decorate the room, get crafts ready etc		
One hour before	Team meeting for prayer and final instructions		
10 minutes before (for 15 minutes)	Children arrive, register and are given a name label—before being taken to their opening activities eg: colouring competition, bouncy castle (available to rent), opening games (see **Ideas Menu** for Easter games, pages 52-54)		
25 minutes Together Time 1	Welcome—introduction of leaders, what's going to happen, rules etc Team challenge (see **Ideas Menu**, page 49) Song (see **Music Spot**, page 49 for song suggestions) Team challenge Memory verse (see **Ideas Menu**, page 49) Song Quiz (see **Ideas Menu**, page 49)		
25 minutes	Crafts (see **Ideas Menu**, pages 50-52) Drink and a snack in groups		
25 minutes Together Time 2	Team challenge Song Bible story (**Talk idea 1**, page 44) Song Prayer (see **Ideas Menu**, page 52) Quiz		
15 minutes	Small-group time (see **Ideas Menu**, page 52)		
25 minutes	Games (see **Ideas Menu**, pages 52-54)—maybe do one big game all together at the end. Promote upcoming events and award any prizes.		

Option B: Four-hour children's event
with parents invited to come and watch performance at end

Gear

- Registration forms, name labels and pens
- Colouring sheets and pencils
- Materials for your games, challenges and crafts
- Visual aids for the Eyewitness accounts
- Memory-verse props
- Small-groups sheets and pencil for each child
- Music and words for songs
- Quiz questions and scoreboard
- Refreshments
- DVD player and screen
- Copies of play scripts
- Publicity for Easter services or events

Time	Activity	✔	Leader
	Tick when materials are ready for each activity		
Before event	Preparation eg: decorate room, get crafts ready etc		
One hour before	Team meeting for prayer and final instructions		
10 minutes before (for 15 minutes)	Children arrive, register and are given a name label—before being taken to their opening activities eg: colouring competition, bouncy castle (available to rent), opening games (see **Ideas Menu** for Easter games, pages 52-54)		
25 minutes Together Time 1	Welcome—introduction of leaders, what's going to happen, rules etc Team challenge (see **Ideas Menu**, page 49) Song (see **Music Spot**, page 49) Team challenge Eyewitness 1—A disciple (see page 46) Prayer (see **Ideas Menu**, page 52) Song		
25 minutes	Crafts (see **Ideas Menu**, pages 50-52) Drink and a snack in groups		
25 minutes Together Time 2	Team challenge Song Eyewitness 2—Peter (see page 46) Team challenge Song Quiz (see **Ideas Menu**, page 49)		
25 minutes	Games (see **Ideas Menu**, pages 52-54)—maybe do one big game all together at the end. Give details about church groups and invite children to come.		
25 minutes Together Time 3	Team challenge Song Memory verse (see **Ideas Menu**, page 49) Team challenge Eyewitness 3—Barabbas (see page 47) Song		
40 minutes	Younger children watch an Easter DVD (see **Ideas Menu**, page 52) Older children rehearse their play (see drama suggestions on pages 60-62) *Optional: some children to ice biscuits/cookies and make props. Alternatively, this could be done in the earlier craft session.*		
25 minutes Together Time 4	Team challenge Song Eyewitness 4—Mary (see page 47) Team challenge Song Quiz		
20 minutes	Small groups (see **Ideas Menu**, page 52)		
25 minutes	Lunch/tea (You may provide something simple eg: hot dogs, crisps/chips, fruit, biscuits/cookies; alternatively your publicity could mention bringing sandwiches.) Towards the end, award prizes and play a quick game with those who have finished.		
30 minutes	Performance—parents come to see the Easter play, along with the memory verse and songs. Light refreshments served. Announcements for other upcoming events.		

Option C: One-and-a-half-hour family fun event

Gear

- Mini eggs
- Materials for your choice of games, challenges and crafts
- Visual aids for the talk
- Wall quiz
- Quiz questions and scoreboard
- Refreshments
- Prizes
- Publicity for Easter services or events

Time	Activity	✔	Leader
	Tick when materials are ready for each activity		
Before event	Preparation eg: decorate room, get games and refreshments ready etc		
One hour before	Team meeting for prayer and final instructions		
10 minutes before (for 15 minutes)	Doors open Mini-egg yes/no game (see **Ideas Menu**, page 54) Easter egg wall quiz (see **Ideas Menu**, page 52)		
3 minutes	Introduction; then split entire group into 4 or 6 teams.		
47 minutes	Family teams rotate around the different Easter-themed side stalls (the team challenges could be used as some of the side stalls). If they complete all of them, they can always go back and try to improve their score.		
15 minutes	Refreshments Smashing egg quiz (see **Ideas Menu**, page 49)		
10 minutes	Bible talk (Talk idea 2, page 45)		
5 minutes	Prizes and announcements		

Talk idea 1

Suitable for children's or family events

You will need to prepare the following props as well as reading through the talk several times so that you are familiar with it.

Gear

▶ Six different kinds of chocolate egg*, five of which have been carefully unwrapped, split in half (use a hot knife and insert along seam), something put in the middle, re-wrapped and boxed. Contents for the eggs are:

- a foil crown
- a plan folded up
- a sad face folded up
- an empty sweet wrapper (It would be best if this matches what should be in the box)
- a coin (eg: £2, $1) or note (eg: £5, $5)

▶ 6 paper plates

▶ Hammer

* You can use chocolate rabbits, or plastic eggs, if you can't find large chocolate eggs.

If you are doing this in a family event, you may want to have copies of Luke's Gospel on the tables. Add some Bible references into your talk and encourage people to follow them. At the end, explain that they can take away the Gospel as a gift, and read it through to find out more.

Bible talk

So what's your favourite Easter egg? Lindt? Mars? Snickers? Have you put your orders in yet? Well, don't worry if you haven't, as I've brought some spares along with me today and we're going to have a cracking time! (Pull out hammer.) **And as we do, we're going to think a little more about the very first Easter.**

> **First egg:** Hold up the box of the first Easter egg and read out what should be inside the egg (eg: mini eggs or chocolate bunnies). Ask a child to come up and crack the egg open. Hold up what is really inside the egg—a foil crown.

Why a crown? Well, the very first Easter week began with a big celebration, as Jesus entered Jerusalem. For three years He had been travelling around, performing miracle after miracle, proving He was God's Son. But the crowds thought He'd just come as their king to rescue them from the Romans—so they went wild when He arrived. They waved palm leaves and covered the road with their coats. But they had got it so wrong. Jesus *was* a rescuing King, but He had come to save them—and us—from something far greater than the Romans. Jesus had come to provide a way for us to be saved from God's punishment, that we deserve.

> **Second egg:** Hold up the box of the second Easter egg and read out what should be inside the egg. Ask a child to come up and crack the egg open. Hold up what is really inside the egg—a plan.

You see, Jesus' death was not a mistake, a horrible accident: it was actually part of God's rescue plan for us. We see evidence of this all through the Easter story. Let me give you some examples. Not only did Jesus know where the donkey would be that He was going to ride, but actually, by riding it, He was keeping a promise that God had made hundreds of years before.

And then, there was the incredible conversation He had with His friends at the special Passover meal a few days later. Imagine you're sat round the tea table, when all of a sudden, instead of someone asking for the ketchup or moaning about the sprouts, they tell you they are about to die and you have to do certain things to remember them. It would be pretty shocking, wouldn't it?! Well, that's exactly what Jesus did. He told His friends that one of them was going to let Him down and that He was going to die. So we know that Jesus' death wasn't an accident. He knew that it was going to happen because it was planned since before the world began. That's how much God cares for us.

> **Third egg:** Hold up the box of the third Easter egg and read out what should be inside the egg. Ask a child to come up and crack the egg open. Hold

up what is really inside the egg—a picture of a sad face.

Well, after the meal, Jesus went to pray and asked His friends to watch and keep guard—but guess what? They didn't—they just slept! And while they slept, Jesus talked to God. In fact He begged God that if there was any way out of His death, to give it to Him. However, Jesus then went on to agree to obey God as He knew it was the only way people could saved—it was the only way people could be forgiven and be made right with God.

Then, just as Jesus had said, He was arrested, and let down by a couple of His best friends in the process. Even though He had never done anything wrong, Jesus was beaten and picked on. He was eventually sentenced to death by the Roman Governor, Pontius Pilate, in the place of a murderer, Barabbas. But remember—Jesus wasn't just dying in Barabbas' place—He was dying in ours too. This was all part of God's rescue plan. Let's find out how…

> **Fourth egg:** Hold up the box of the fourth Easter egg and read out what should be inside the egg. Ask a child to come up and crack the egg open. Hold up what is really inside the egg—an empty sweet wrapper.

Sorry—I ate that earlier! The sweet is finished, it's no more. And do you know, Jesus shouted out "It is finished!" when He was on the cross. Not because the sweet had gone or because the pain was over, but because His job of saving people was finished. Through Him, the punishment had been taken for the wrong things we say and think and do. King Jesus was cut off from God on the cross so we don't have to be. He died so we can be forgiven instead of punished; friends with God instead of enemies with God. No one else could do that for us… and no one else could do what He did next.

> **Fifth egg:** Hold up the box of the fifth Easter egg and read out what should be inside the egg. Ask a child to come up and crack the egg open. Hold up what is really inside the egg—nothing!

That's right—this one is completely empty—just like the tomb on that Sunday morning 2000 years ago. It was proof that Jesus was alive. Later, Jesus' friends met Him in all sorts of places—in a house, along a road, on a beach. They ate with Him, chatted with Him, and touched Him. Over 500 people saw He was alive. But for now the proof was the empty tomb, the stone rolled away, the grave clothes folded. Jesus had risen again because He has power over all things. Nothing could beat Him. And because Jesus had new life, we can too. We can have 100% certainty of heaven if we're a follower of Jesus. No one else can offer that.

> **Sixth egg:** Hold up the box of the sixth Easter egg and read out what should be inside the egg. Ask a child to come up and crack the egg open. Hold up what is really inside the egg—money (a coin or note).

Wow! That's better than expected, isn't it! Do you know what? On that Sunday morning we read that Jesus' friends were expecting to find a dead body—but instead they saw an angel and discovered something much better than they expected. And we can have a similar experience, for God gives us something more wonderful than we can ever imagine, something we'll never deserve—He gives us access to Him, He offers us friendship for ever, day in and day out, good times and bad. He promises us eternal life if we accept His offer of forgiveness.

Now the question is… are we going to be more excited about this than munching our Easter eggs? Now Jesus has taken the punishment we deserve, we know we can be friends with God and live for ever with Him. So will you accept His offer and give Him your love and praise? Will you say sorry for the times you've ignored Him and let Him down, and will you thank Him for dying in your place? Will you turn to Him and trust in Him, seeking to listen to Him and put Him first, as He forgives you and changes you? Will you at least think a little more about it this Easter?

Talk idea 2
Suitable for children's events

You will need to collect the following things as well as reading through the talk several times so that you are familiar with it.

Gear

▶ Enough copies of the Eyewitness scripts (pages 46-47) for each person taking part
▶ Props and costumes if required

One person could play all four roles or you could have four different actors. The eyewitness accounts could be used in three different ways:

1. All four parts in the same teaching slot, with a summary at the end.

2. Re-told by the characters, who are then "hot-seated" as the children ask them questions.

3. Re-told by the characters with the main leader adding a link after each one.

Details of these three options are given on pages 47-48.

Drama

Eyewitness accounts

(See page 47 for a choice of teaching slots to use after these eyewitness accounts. The person/people acting these roles may like to wear a simple Bible costume.)

Eyewitness 1—A disciple
(Palm Sunday)

Howdys! It was Sunday when we finally arrived in Bethphage and Bethany on the Mount of Olives. We were all heading on our way to Jerusalem, along with everyone else it seemed, to celebrate the Passover festival later on that week.

The crowds were pushing in on us—shoving us from every side. I guess it was only natural since we were travelling there with Jesus. You know about Jesus, don't you? You know—the one who turned water into wine, made blind people see, calmed storms and fed 5000 people. The miracle worker, the great teacher, the perfect man, the one they said was from God—and the one I had spent the last three years hanging round with. That's right, I'm one of His gang.

Well anyway, Jesus didn't seem fazed by the attention; instead He called me and one of the other disciples and said: "Go into the village. As soon as you enter it, you'll find a young donkey which has never given anyone a ride. Untie it and bring it to me." He also told us, if anyone asked us what we were doing, we just had to explain that Jesus needed it and would return it soon.

We went off right away and sure enough, just like he said, there was this young donkey tied outside the front door of a house. As we were untying it, some people asked us what we were up to, but when we gave Jesus' explanation they were fine with it. As we led it back to Jesus and the others, I couldn't help wondering what was going to happen next. Was Jesus going to show us He was God's King, like the old writings had said? Was He on His way to Jerusalem to rescue us from the Romans? Were we going to be free at last from them?

We took the donkey to Jesus, put our coats on its back and then helped Jesus to climb on. People all around me started to cheer and celebrate. It really did look like Jesus was God's King, just like we'd hoped—He was doing exactly what had been written in the Old Testament.

As Jesus rode into Jerusalem, some threw their coats on the floor like a red carpet; others started to pull off palm leaves and wave them. "Hurray! Here comes our king on the donkey. Hosanna, Hosanna to Jesus the King. Praise God for sending Him!"

What a fantastic day! What we didn't know was it was the start of an incredible week, which would be full of highs and lows, but more about that later...

Eyewitness 2—Peter
(Arrest and denial)

Alright! I'm Peter—or Simon Peter if my mum's around! I don't want to brag, but I have this one awesome friend—His name is Jesus. Ever since my bro, Andrew, pointed me in His direction three years ago, I've gone here, there and everywhere with Jesus—listening to Him, chatting to Him, watching Him, and if I'm honest, sometimes arguing with Him. You see, I like to think I always know best—the problem is, I don't, and the last few weeks have shown that time and again!

Well anyway, a week or so ago we had this massive meal together—me, Jesus, my brother Andrew and the others in our gang. We were celebrating the Passover festival—thanking God for how He'd rescued us in the past—when all of a sudden Jesus told us He was about to die. He said that after He had gone we should eat bread and drink wine together and remember that He chose to die in our place, to take God's punishment for us.

To be honest, we didn't believe Him. He had said things like this before—about dying and coming back to life on the third day—but we weren't convinced, and I had told Him as much before. We started to argue with Him and I told Him how I was willing to do anything to protect Him—but He wasn't having any of it—in fact He said I'd do the opposite. He said I'd let Him down three times before the cock crowed. Surely not! But there was time to discuss further as Jesus told us it was time to go for a walk to the Garden of Gethsemane.

Well I dunno about you, but after a big feast, I'm always wiped out and need a quick power nap to recover. The problem was when we got to the garden, Jesus asked us not to sleep, but instead keep watch for the soldiers while He prayed. I wanted so much to stay awake—to wait for my friend, to prove I could protect Him—but I couldn't... I was just tooooooo tired. (Yawn and stretch.)

Jesus woke me and the others up with a shake: "Please watch and wait. Please pray." He looked so sad—like He'd been crying. Well, I tried again to stay awake—but do you know what? I fell asleep again! Rubbish! Rubbish! Rubbish!

Jesus woke us up as the soldiers and religious leaders walked towards Him with swords and clubs. I tried to stop them; I thought I knew best, but Jesus didn't want me to fight and so He allowed them to arrest Him and lead Him away. I followed in the shadows, afraid they would arrest me also, but wanting to see what would happen to Jesus. As they questioned Him and bullied Him, a few people saw me watching and said I was His friend. But I denied everything. Time and again I let Him down... and then the cock crowed, just like He had said. I had failed Him, and now He was about to die.

Eyewitness 3—Barabbas
(Crucifixion)

As I sat in my cold, dark, damp prison cell waiting to be killed for the murder I had committed, I began to hear what sounded like a very large crowd shouting. As the shouting grew louder and louder, I realised they were shouting MY name! My name!! "Release Barabbas, free Barabbas, release Barabbas!" they cried time and time again. But why? I'd committed murder; I was due to be killed on a cross that day, along with two other criminals.

"Kill him! Nail him to a cross! Nail him to a cross!" I heard the crowd shout. "Nail who to a cross?" I asked myself. "If they want me freed, who are they going to crucify?" The noise outside grew even louder and louder and the shouts of "Kill him! Nail him to a cross!" grew even more persistent.

Finally, when the shouting became almost deafening, a cheer erupted—and then I began to hear my name again: "Barabbas, Barabbas, Barabbas..." What on earth was going on?

Just then a guard came in and unlocked the chains I was in. He told me that I was free, that Jesus was going to be put to death in my place.

Jesus? JESUS? Everyone had heard of Jesus—Jesus, the one who had turned water into wine, made blind people see, calmed storms and fed 5000 people. The miracle worker, the great teacher, the perfect man, the one they said was from God. Why would they want to kill Him and free me? It didn't make sense. And why would Jesus allow it and die in my place? Surely there must be more to it!

Eyewitness 4—Mary
(Resurrection)

Friday was a horrible day. The Roman soldiers had nailed Jesus to a cross and left Him there to die. Some of them gambled for His clothes, while others shouted and made fun of Him. Why? Why were they doing this? Why were they being so cruel? Why were they killing Jesus, the miracle worker, the great teacher, the perfect man, God's Son, my friend? And why did Jesus see it as the way of rescue? Was it just Barabbas' place He was dying in? What was going to happen next?

My mind was spilling over with questions but my heart ached so much it hurt—especially when Jesus

cried out "It is finished" and died. I now know He wasn't talking about His life, but rather the fact He had taken God's punishment for all of us. He had died in our places, not just in place of Barabbas. But on Friday, when I heard Him say that, I just wept even more.

As they took Him off the cross, Joseph offered for his tomb to be used as Jesus' grave. We wrapped Jesus' body in a cloth, put Him in the cave, and pushed a huge stone in front. The Roman soldiers stood guard. I thought that was it, we'd never see Jesus again. How wrong I was!

On Sunday morning, another Mary, Joanna and I decided to go and put some perfume on Jesus' body to stop it smelling. We weren't sure how we would get into the cave, with that huge boulder in front, but hoped we'd manage somehow. However, we didn't need to worry, for as we came closer to the tomb, there was loud banging and crashing. It was an earthquake. Everything shook; then all we saw was an angel. He rolled back the stone and sat on it. He looked like lightning and his clothes were as white as snow. The soldiers had collapsed on the ground in shock. And then the angel spoke...

He told us not to be afraid! He knew that we were looking for Jesus, but told us that we wouldn't find Him in the tomb—it was empty. Jesus had risen just like He said He would. The angel instructed us to go and tell Jesus' other special friends and get ready, because we were going to see the risen Jesus ourselves soon. And do you know what? He was right—we did. We spoke with Him, touched Him, and ate with Him. Jesus is alive! He is more powerful than anything because He is God! And not only can we be forgiven because He died in our place, taking God's punishment for us, but we can also have new life in Him—be His friend forever and go to heaven, all because Jesus beat death and came back to life.

Variation 1

All four eyewitness accounts in the same teaching slot, followed by this summary:

Wow! Did you get all that? Did you hear who Jesus is? He's the one who had turned water into wine, made blind people see, calmed storms and fed 5000 people. Jesus is a miracle worker and the only perfect man ever as He's God's Son, God's special King. And more than that, Jesus' death was all part of a plan.

You see, we all do things that make God angry—we ignore Him and disobey Him, we say, think and do things that are wrong. We let Him down, just like Peter did in the story and so we deserve to be punished by God. But because God loves us so much, He sent Jesus to die, so that He could die in our place, not just Barabbas', and take the punishment we deserve from God, so that we can be forgiven, become His friends and live for ever with Him.

Wasn't it brilliant to hear from Mary that Jesus had power even over death? And that because He rose again we have a hope that we can also have eternal life, all because of what He's done. So will you say sorry to God for the times you haven't treated Him the right way, and for the times you've said wrong or done wrong or thought wrong? Have you thanked Him for dying in your place, and taking your punishment to provide the way for you to be friends with Him. Will you ask Him to forgive you and change you, and help you live in a way that pleases Him?

Variation 2

Re-told by the characters, who are then "hot-seated" as the children ask them questions.

Hot seating is where people act out characters from a story, the children ask them questions and the characters have to answer them in as much detail as possible, from what we're told in the Bible.

Before the characters are interviewed, it is important to tell the children that the answers will be based on the Bible. If a question is asked for which there is no information in the Bible, the character will need to explain that they cannot answer.

Afterwards, "hot-seat" a leader. Begin by asking them what they believe about the first Easter and how Jesus' coming has made a difference in their life. Then allow children to ask related questions.

Variation 3

Re-told by the characters with the main leader adding a link after each one.

 After the disciple's speech

Sounds pretty exciting, doesn't it! A bit like when a celebrity is in town with all that pushing and shoving. Can anyone tell me why the people were so excited to see Jesus? (Take responses eg: He was a miracle-worker; they thought He had come to rescue them from the Romans.)

The crowd had got some of it right—Jesus was a very special King. I mean, look at the way He knew about the donkey—wasn't that amazing! I wonder what else He knew? And what His friend meant when He said it would be an incredible week... Guess we'll have to wait to find out...

 After Peter's speech

Oh dear, Peter seems to have messed up a bit, doesn't he? Are you ever like that, telling lies to try and get yourself out of trouble? Whether it's lies or something else, the Bible tells us we all say, think and do wrong things. All of us put ourselves first instead of living God's way, and the Bible teaches that we deserve to be punished for that.

But that's why Jesus came. That's why He knew He was going to die in our place. Jesus came to rescue us so we can be forgiven by God and become His friend for ever—that's what He meant at the meal with Peter.

 After Barabbas' speech

So that's it, is it? Jesus sent to die in the place of a murderer, even though He hadn't done anything wrong. Does it seem strange to you? Well, Jesus died in our places too as it was the only way for us to be made right with God. He was our perfect substitute. Have you thanked Him for doing that? Have you said sorry for the times you've let Him down and ignored Him? Have you asked Him to forgive you and help you follow Him? If you haven't, you're a bit like the leaders in the story who rejected Jesus. That means you are saying "no" to God and His rescue plan, and so you won't be saved from God's punishment.

But that can change, as Jesus died to make a way of rescue available for everybody—so why not chat to one of the leaders here today?

 After Mary's speech

Isn't that amazing! Jesus came back to life; nothing's more powerful than Him. And do you know what? If you are forgiven by Him, you'll have new life too. You'll be His friend for ever— you'll go to heaven when you die. Mary and the other women obeyed the angel when he said "Go and tell" because they believed in Jesus. They made sure they went and told others the good news. And you can do the same. If you've asked Jesus to forgive you and are living with Jesus as your King, you'll want to do what God wants and tell others about Him.

IDEAS MENU

Five team challenges

These can be used to create team spirit and an enthusiastic environment. If you have divided the children into teams, it's good to get a representative up from each one.

These also work well as some of the side-stall games for a family fun event.

Rabbit racing

Gear
- Card / card stock ears (see page 87) stapled to a card headband, one per team
- A woolly pom-pom per team
- A piece of string per team

One volunteer from each team puts on a headband, with the pom-pom tied around their bottom. Race a certain distance and back, doing bunny hops.

Scrambled eggs

Gear
- Eggs
- A very large tarpaulin

Two children are chosen from each team. They stand opposite their partner, about 1m apart. They are to throw the egg (raw!) over to their partner. If it is caught, each to take a small step back; if dropped, they sit down. Continue until all are eliminated.

Easter-egg nose rally

Gear
- Lots of real eggs

Eggs must be rolled around a course, only using the nose. In this games, is does not matter if the eggs are raw or hard-boiled.

Flipping in the dark

Gear
- Blindfolds
- Two frying pans
- Plastic lids to use as "pancakes" (eg: from plastic tubs or sandwich boxes)

Choose a volunteer per team. See how many times they can flip the "pancake" in one minute.

Guess the mini eggs in the jar

Gear
- A jar
- Lots of chocolate mini eggs

Children to guess how many eggs there are. The closest guess wins the jar and all the mini eggs in it.

Music spot

Choose from the following song suggestions for the various song slots.

Who is this man? (track 23) of *The King, the snake and the promise* CD

How cool is that! (track 4) of Johnny Burns' *How cool is that!* CD

Jesus is alive today (track 12) of the *Promises, promises* CD

Are you ready? (track 7) of the *Promises, promises* CD

What sort of King? (track 23) of the *Meet the King* CD

My King (track 12) of the *Earth Movers* CD

Memory verse

For Christ died for sins once for all, the righteous for the unrighteous, to bring you to God. 1 Peter 3 v 18a (NIV)

Gear
- A large, card / card stock Easter egg, with the memory verse words clearly written on it. Cut it up into jigsaw pieces.

Have the different "egg" pieces stuck on a board or a wall. Ask a volunteer from each team to go and try and quickly assemble the egg. Time them. Then read through the verse. Make sure you explain **righteous** (pleasing to God, right in His sight) and **unrighteous** (missing the mark—maybe use a target board to show this).

Gradually remove the "egg" pieces, asking the teams to repeat the verse back to you each time.

Smashing egg quiz

Gear
- Paper-maché eggs, made in advance, with points inside (see below)
- A range of questions based on the main teaching points and what has been covered in the session

Use the quiz to reinforce what has been taught in a fun way and to help teams score points. If the children

answer the question correctly, they are to come up, and choose a giant egg. They then have to smash it in 5 seconds (everyone else doing a countdown) and pull the points out. Make sure the questions are clear and pitched at all ages.

To make the eggs you will need:

- Large, oval balloons (one per egg)
- Newspaper
- Watered-down PVA (white) glue
- Masking tape
- White paint
- Pieces of paper with points written on them (a different number of points on each piece)

1. Tear several newspaper pages into strips, about 3cm wide and 20cm long.

2. Blow up the balloons and tie them closed.

3. Dip the newspaper strips into the glue and spread them onto the balloon. Completely cover the balloon, leaving a small hole at the top to remove the balloon. Complete at least two more layers and leave to dry.

4. Once the paper-maché is dry, pop the balloon and remove it through the opening you left at the top.

5. Paint each "egg" white; then poke a piece of paper with points on it inside each egg.

Craft

Easter plates

Gear
- Paper plates (2 per child)
- Scissors
- Felt-tip pens or coloured crayons
- Stapler

1. Colour the centre of a paper plate.

2. Cut the paper plate in half. The two halves will be the rabbit's ears.

3. Using a new paper plate, cut a wedge (about ¼ of the plate) out of the paper plate. The large part of the plate will be the rabbit's face.

4. Staple the ears to the face.

5. Decorate the plate with crayons, or felt-tip pens. Don't forget to draw whiskers!

Cooking

Cookie baking

Gear
- Baking trays
- Easter cutters
- 175g / 6oz plain flour
- 100g / 4oz butter or margarine
- 50g / 2oz caster sugar
- Paper plates

1. Preheat oven to 190°C (375°F, Gas mark 5).

2. Cream the butter/margarine and caster sugar together until they are light and fluffy.

3. Stir in the flour and, once mixed, knead the dough together until it forms a ball. Add a sprinkle of flour if the dough is at all sticky.

4. Roll out the dough on a lightly floured surface until it is about 5mm (1/4 inch) thick.

5. Cut out the dough using your chosen cutter.

6. Place the cookies on a floured baking tray and bake in the centre of the oven for 15 minutes or until golden brown.

7. Make an Easter plate while the children wait for the cookies to cook.

Cooking

Chocolate eggs

Gear
- Chocolate
- Easter-egg moulds (large if children are making one egg each or small if they are making several)
- Wooden spoons
- Bowls
- Teaspoons
- Large paintbrushes
- Icing pens (available from cook shops, optional)
- Shredded Wheat breakfast cereal (optional)
- Paper cupcake/muffin cases (optional)

1. Break up chocolate and melt.

2. Use a large brush to paint melted chocolate onto the inside of the egg moulds.

3. Once you have coated the whole of the inside of the mould with chocolate, place it into the fridge for five minutes.

4. "Re-paint" the whole of the inside of the mould with chocolate a couple of times, placing it into the fridge for five minutes in between painting each layer of chocolate.

5. When the chocolate is set (at least ten minutes in fridge), turn the mould upside down on a table and gently tap to remove the egg halves.

ONE DAY WONDERS

6. If making large eggs, use a little melted chocolate to stick the two halves of the egg together. The egg can be decorated with an icing pen if wanted.

7. If the children have made small eggs, they can make a "nest" as follows: In a large bowl of melted chocolate, stir in broken up strips of Shredded Wheat cereal (mixture will be very stiff and just sticks together).

8. Press the mixture of chocolate and Shredded Wheat into cupcake/muffin cases to look like a bird's nest. When set, place three or four of their small eggs into each nest.

Craft
Egg decorating

Gear
- Hard-boiled eggs
- Crayons
- Crepe paper
- Spoons
- Foil
- Hot water
- White vinegar

1. Beforehand, make dye by putting strips of crepe paper (darker colors seem to work better) into a container. Cover in hot water with 2tsp of white vinegar. Leave for a few hours.

2. Using crayons, draw designs onto the eggs. Heavier lines will show up more after dying than thin lines.

3. Using spoons, put eggs into dye—cover as much of the egg as wanted.

4. Leave in dye for a few minutes; then put into another bowl if another colour is desired.

5. Lift egg out with a spoon and place on a piece of foil to dry.

Craft
Egg heads

Gear
- Polystyrene eggs (available in craft shops)
- PVA (white) glue
- Googly eyes
- Scraps of fabric or "funky foam"
- Stick-on jewels
- Craft pom-poms, feathers, etc

Children use their own choice of the available materials to decorate their egg head.

Craft
Mini Easter gardens

Gear
- Plastic containers (eg: the small salad boxes you get in your local supermarket)
- Film canisters (or the centres from Kinder Eggs)
- Compost
- Cress seeds or grass seed
- Pebbles
- Craft flowers
- Ice-lolly sticks (available from craft shops, 2 per child)
- PVA (white) glue

1. Half fill the plastic container with compost.

2. For Jesus' empty tomb, half bury an empty film canister and put more compost on top of it to make it look as if it is in the side of a hill.

3. Put a pebble by the open end of the canister.

4. Sow the cress seeds and lightly water.

5. Arrange the craft flowers.

6. Stick the lollipop sticks together in a cross shape and plant in the far corner of the container.

Craft
Egg cups

Gear
- Plain wooden egg cups
- Paintbrushes
- Acrylic paint
- Water in water pots (to clean brushes)

Children paint their egg cups with their own designs.

Craft
Egg t-shirts

Gear
- Plain white t-shirts
- Egg templates (egg outline from page 88 or 89 copied onto thin card / card stock and cut out to make templates)
- Fabric pens or paints
- Scrap paper or newspaper

1. Give children a t-shirt each.

2. Ask children to put a sheet of newspaper or some scrap paper inside their t-shirts.

3. Children draw round the egg template on their t-shirt.

4. Decorate with dots, stripes, etc using fabric pens or paints.

Craft

Palm Sunday flags

Gear

▶ Sheets of white paper (A4 / US letter)
▶ Sellotape (transparent tape)
▶ Pieces of coloured paper (A5 / Half US letter)
▶ Felt-tip pens
▶ Stickers
▶ Glitter glue

1. Children are to roll up the white paper tightly and tape together. It is better if this is done diagonally.

2. Then selloptape on a piece of coloured paper.

3. Decorate the flag with pictures of Easter-related things.

4. Add a little sparkle with glitter glue and stickers.

Teach us to pray

Prayer

Gear

▶ Lots of stones
▶ Lots of felt-tip pens

Brainstorm with the children words to describe Jesus' death and resurrection, eg: amazing, powerful, loving.

Ask the children to choose one word and write it on their stone. Encourage them to take the stone home and keep it by their bed to remind them to thank Jesus for what He did.

Then pray with the children, as they hold the rocks in their hands: **Father God, thank You for sending Jesus to come and die in our place. Thank You that You want to forgive us even though we don't deserve it. Please help us understand what it means to follow You. Amen.**

Small groups

Small groups

Options A and B both include time for the children to be split into small groups where they can think about the teaching they have heard. We suggest that these groups meet for 15 minutes, just after the main teaching slot.

Pages 57-59 include copies of fun sheets to use in these groups. The sheets have been designed for three age groups: 4-7s (Reception to Year 2)—page 57, 7-9s (Years 3-4)—page 58, 9-11s (Years 5-6)—page 59. With the older groups, you may also choose to have Bibles available so that they can read for themselves some of the Bible story they have heard. If you don't have sufficient Bibles available, you can copy the relevant text from www.biblegateway.com to print out your own sheets.

On pages 55-56 there are notes to help the leaders of the small groups. Please give copies of these to each small-group leader in advance, so that they can prepare thoroughly. This is particularly important if the small groups are being led by an inexperienced leader or helper (which may be the case if you have a small team and a large number of children).

DVDs

Easter DVDs

Choose from the following DVDs:

The Miracle Maker (ISBN 0564042854)

Easter Storykeepers (ISBN VD722)

He is Risen! (Animated stories from the New Testament, ASIN B0006UKLXU)

Games

Easter-egg wall quiz

Gear

▶ Cropped pictures of chocolate Easter egg boxes (so only a small section can be seen). Make the pictures as large as possible (eg: A3 / twice US letter) and number each one.

Display the pictures around the room. Teams/families have to try and work out what kinds of Easter egg they are pictures of.

Games

What's in the box?

Gear

▶ A large box decorated in Easter-themed paper
▶ A selection of items that are wrapped so that they can be felt but not seen, eg:
  • Bread roll
  • Toy sword
  • A cross
  • Easter egg
  • A stone

Sit the children in a circle and take out the first item. Pass it around the circle. The children can try to guess what it is. Unwrap the item to find out if they are right.

Egg and spoon relay race

Gear
- Wooden spoons
- Chocolate eggs
- Obstacles (eg: play tunnels, tables, cones...)

Split the children into teams. Give each team an egg and a spoon. Each child has to go through the obstacle course and race back to their team while carrying the egg on the spoon. Repeat until all team members have completed the course.

Alternatively, the children could just pass the egg on the spoon all the way down the line to the end. The person at the end then has to run to the front and start passing it back once more. Continue until the team is back in its original position. You could tell the children to begin again if the egg is dropped.

Easter Pictionary

Gear
- List of Easter-related words and phrases (eg: donkey, bread, cup of wine, garden, crown of thorns, soldier, nails, sword, stone, angel)
- Plenty of paper
- Felt-tip pens

Split children into two teams. One volunteer from each team is shown (or whispered) a word which he/she must draw on the paper for the rest of the team to guess. How many words will the group manage to guess within two minutes?

Easter Bunny says

Played like "Simon Says". Choose a leader or child to be the "Easter Bunny". If they say "Easter Bunny says hop on one foot", the children must hop on one foot. If they say "Stop", the children are to keep hopping on one foot until they say "Easter Bunny says stop". Repeat for additional activities such as taking one baby step forward, stepping backwards, turning around, sitting down. Sometimes Easter Bunny will say "Easter Bunny says" and sometimes he/she won't.

Pin the stone on the tomb

Gear
- A picture of a tomb/cave
- A picture of a stone
- Blu-Tack reuseable adhesive
- Blindfold (eg: scarf or airline sleep mask)

Blindfold the player, spin them around and let them try to stick the stone over the mouth of the tomb. Give a prize for the player that gets the closest.

Remind the children that the tomb was empty on the first Easter Sunday because Jesus wasn't dead any more. He had risen.

Easter-egg hunt

Gear
- Lots of wrapped mini eggs or plastic eggs

Hide the eggs before the event. Split the children into teams, giving each one a base. Have the children hunt for the eggs. Then have children go back to their base and count how many eggs the whole group has. The group with the highest number of eggs collected gets to eat theirs first.

Musical Easter eggs

Gear
- Giant cardboard Easter eggs
- CD player and CD

Spread the cardboard eggs out on the floor. When the music is playing, the children are to move around the room. When the music stops, they need to stand on an egg. If they fail to find one, they're out. Remove one or more eggs and continue to play.

Palm, palm, donkey

The children sit in a circle. One child is "it" and hops around the circle tapping each child on the head and saying "Palm, palm, palm..." until he/she finally says, "DONKEY". Both children "gallop" around the circle trying to reach the empty spot first.

Bunny-hop relay

Gear
- An Easter egg per team

Children divide into teams. Give each team an egg. Have one child from each team place the egg between their legs and hop to the end of the room and back. They sit down and the next team member goes. This is repeated until one team are all sitting.

Soldier chain tag

Gear
- A toy Roman soldier's helmet

A child begins by being "the soldier". Give them the helmet to wear. Everyone tries to avoid getting tagged by soldier. However if they are, they have to hold hands with others who've been arrested. The chain should grow longer and longer, until only one person is left. They become the "soldier" for the next game.

Capture the Easter flag

Gear
- 2 flags with Easter pictures (eg: a palm leaf, an angel). See page 52 for how to make the flags.

Divide children into two teams, lined up on opposite sides of the playing space and numbered. Put the flags on the ground in the middle. When a child's number is called, they run, pick up a flag and try to get back to their line without being tagged. Call two numbers at a time to encourage strategy and excitement.

Spot the character

Gear
- Newspapers
- Tape
- Cotton balls
- Straws
- Scrap materials
- Scissors

Split into teams. Everyone makes their own version of a character from the Easter Story, eg: roman soldier, one of the women, a donkey! Award points for team work, creativity, humour etc.

The mystery of the missing eggs

Gear
- A basket of mini eggs
- Blindfold (eg: a scarf or airline sleep mask)

The players form a circle with one child in the middle as "the Easter Bunny". Blindfold them and place the basket in front of them. Choose a volunteer to try and creep up, take a mini egg, and sit back down with the mini egg under their leg. Then the children chant: "Easter Bunny, Easter Bunny, where's your egg? Somebody stole it from your basket!" The Easter Bunny then has three guesses to find the child who is sitting on the missing egg. If they guess correctly, they get to eat a mini egg from their basket! Swap volunteers and repeat.

Egghead

Gear
- Three eggs—one hard-boiled, two raw
- Bowl

Put the eggs in a bowl. Choose a volunteer (a leader if you think this might upset a child) to pick one out and smash it over their head. If they get the hard-boiled one, they get a prize.

Easter-egg bowling match

Gear
- Painted hard-boiled eggs
- One plain hard-boiled egg

Give each child a different colour egg. Place the unpainted egg on the floor about 2 metres away from the children. They have to roll their eggs towards the unpainted one. Whoever's egg is rolled closest to the unpainted one wins that round.

The egg case

Gear
- Newspapers
- Sellotape (transparent tape)
- Straws
- A4 / US letter card
- Scissors
- Strings
- Balloons
- Eggs

Divide the children into small groups. Each group has to create a way to safely transport a raw egg from a table to the floor without breaking. Award prizes for ingenuity and keeping the egg intact.

Yes/No

Gear
- Wrapped mini chocolate eggs

Give each participant 5 mini eggs (or dried peas if you prefer). They have to walk around asking others questions. If the person questioned answers "yes" or "no", they have to hand over an egg.

Leading a small group—notes for leaders

- Sit the children in a circle.

Ice-breaker:

- Start by introducing yourself and maybe say your favourite chocolate bar / colour / food.

- Ask children to do the same.

- Ask them what they have liked best so far today… and maybe share with them your favourite bit too!

Fun sheet:

- Explain that we are going to be thinking about the story we just heard.

- Give out a sheet each and pencil or felt-tip pen. Ask them to write their name on the sheet.

- Work through the questions one at a time, using the attached notes to help you. Encourage the children to talk about each question together, rather than racing ahead.

- Encourage them to complete the colouring and puzzle on the back at home. If they are coming to another event at church, or are a member of a weekly church club, then ask them to bring the sheet back and show you.

Memory verse:

If you have extra time at the end of the sheet, remind the children of the memory verse: "For Christ died for sins once for all, the righteous for the unrighteous, to bring you to God." 1 Peter 3 v 18a

There are a number of ways that you can practise the memory verse:

- Start small, build up
- Use actions or have pictures/symbols instead of, or as well as, words
- Jigsaw puzzle or a code
- Word-cards / balloons (could mix order)—gradually take away or pop balloons
- March it / clap it
- Rap or song

Notes on questions for 4-7s (Reception to Year 2)

1. Circle which events in Jesus' life proved He was God's King. Tell your leader why.

Question 1 is pretty straightforward. Don't forget to sell it to them eg: "Who here is clever enough to remember from the story…?" The pictures are: Zacchaeus, Feeding of the 5000, Calming of the storm. Remind the children that here Jesus showed He had power over weather; power to provide for people and power to change people—what a superhero!

2. Who was set free? What had he done wrong?

Ask the children if they can remember who was the baddie in the story, who was set free—you may need to prompt them eg: "sounds a bit like 'Barry'". After the children have filled in what Barabbas had done wrong, it would be good to point out that even though we may not be exactly the same, we do still do wrong things… AND think wrong things… AND say wrong things… AND disobey God… and so we deserve to be punished by God. Link to when we disobey our teachers/parents— they punish us because we deserve it.

3. Who died in his place?

Nice, easy one that pretty much everyone should be able to answer… JESUS!

4. Who else did Jesus die for? Why?

The 4th question is straightforward, but it would be useful to link back to the fact that we *all* deserve to be punished, but Jesus took God's punishment for us. He died in our place so we can be forgiven and become His friend for ever.

5. How did Jesus coming back to life make people feel? And you?

Run through what the different expressions are on the funsheet. Maybe make the faces yourself or get the children to do so. After they have completed how others felt, ask them to think about how they feel about Jesus coming back from the dead … and then get them to look up and show you that face.

Notes on questions for 7-9s (Years 3 and 4)

1. Can you think of three ways we know Jesus is the Son of God from today's story?

Question 1 is really asking for examples of Jesus' miracles which are touched on in the different eyewitness accounts, and maybe even His birth and teachings. The fact that Jesus knew He was going to die and kept fulfilling different prophecies is further evidence, as was the fact that not even death could conquer Him. If the children struggle, mention some examples, eg: Zacchaeus, calming of the storm, feeding of the 5000, healing someone. Remind the children that Jesus showed He had power over weather and illness; power to provide for people; power to change people; power over death.

2. What had Jesus done wrong? What about us—what have we done wrong?

Remind the children how we've seen Jesus prove that He is God's Son and should be obeyed. Jesus is the only perfect person ever to live—this is important as it meant He really was God and was the only one who could die in our place. Explain that whether they write a few things or lots, they do wrong. Even though we may not be exactly the same, we do still do wrong things… AND think wrong things… AND say wrong things… AND disobey God… and so we deserve to be punished by God.

3. Whose place did Jesus die in and why?

Explain that those who ignore/disobey God deserve to be punished, but because God is loving, He wanted to provide people with a way out, a rescue plan. Jesus took God's punishment for us. He died in our place so we can be forgiven and become His friend for ever.

4. Look at some of the ways Jesus showed He was alive again. Which of these would help you?

Remind the children that not even death is stronger than Jesus—and if we are His friends, we can live for ever with Him. The pictures are: empty tomb, Jesus appearing to people, Jesus eating and drinking with His friends. Ask the children which helps them understand Jesus had come back to life. Ask them to explain why, and share which things help you and why.

5. How did the resurrection make different people feel? And you?

Run through what the different expressions on the funsheet are. Maybe pull the faces yourself or get the children to do so. After they have completed how others felt, ask them to think about how they feel about Jesus coming back from the dead … and then look up and show you that face.

Notes on questions for 9-11s (Years 5 and 6)

1. What was surprising about what happened to Jesus? So why was Jesus not surprised?

The surprise factor of Jesus—the perfect one, God's Son, the miracle worker followed by crowds—being arrested should contrast sharply with the fact He didn't struggle and actually knew about it all. It was planned to the tiniest detail since before time began!

2. Lots of people let Jesus down that first Easter. When and how do you let God down?

Interestingly most of the people go against Jesus out of fear or pride. Why not give some up-to-date, relevant scenarios where that still happens. It may be good to point out, whether they write a few things or lots, even though we may not be exactly the same, we do still do wrong things… AND think wrong things… AND say wrong things… AND disobey God… and so we deserve to be punished by God. Link to when we disobey our teachers/parents, they punish us because we deserve it (an opportunity to recap on yesterday).

3. Who did Jesus die for… and why?

The third question is straightforward, but it would be useful to link back to the fact that we all deserve to be punished, and yet Jesus took God's punishment for us. He died in our place so we can be forgiven and become His friend for ever.

4. What evidence is there that Jesus died and rose again?

For question 4, remind the children that not even death is stronger than Jesus—and if we are His friends, we can live for ever with Him. Link to the prophecies and eyewitness accounts eg: people seeing, touching and eating with Jesus, etc. You may want to tell the children that many of Jesus' followers were put to death for insisting that He had come back to life again. They wouldn't have been willing to die for something they weren't sure of.

5. How does it affect you, knowing Jesus beat even death, is alive for ever and offers us forgiveness?

You may find it useful to tell a bit of your own testimony, before getting the children to think what difference it makes at school, on the footy pitch / sports field etc.

ONE DAY WONDERS

EASTER EGGSPERIENCE

For Christ died for sins once for all, the righteous for the unrighteous, to bring you to God.

1 Peter 3 v 18a

1. Circle the things in Jesus' life that proved He was God's King. Tell your leader why.

2. Who was set free? What had he done wrong?

B _ r _ b b _ s
F _ g h t _ n g and M _ r d _ r

3. Who died in his place?

4. Who else did Jesus die for? Why?

Bad people   Good people   Everyone

5. How did Jesus coming back to life make people feel?

And you?

EASTER EGGSPERIENCE

Soldiers led Jesus into a courtyard. Later, they led Him to the place where He was crucified.

Follow the path.

After Jesus died, He was buried in a stone tomb. But He didn't stay dead! God brought Jesus back to life.

Colour in the picture.

EASTER EGGSPERIENCE

For Christ died for sins once for all, the righteous for the unrighteous, to bring you to God.

1 Peter 3 v 18a

1. Can you think of three ways we know Jesus is the Son of God from today's story?

    1.

    2.

    3.

2. What had Jesus done wrong? What about us—what have we done wrong?

3. Whose place did Jesus die in and why?

4. Look at some of the ways Jesus showed He was alive again. Which of these would help you?

5. How did the resurrection make different people feel?

And you?

EASTER EGGSPERIENCE

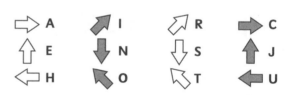

When the soldiers came to arrest Jesus, He could have escaped – but He didn't!

Crack the code to see why.

_ _ _ _ _ _ _ _ _ _ _ _ _ _

_ _ _ _ _ _ _

Jesus didn't fight back because He chose to die as our Rescuer.

Three days after Jesus died, some of His friends went to the tomb where He had been buried. Two angels surprised them by saying:

_ _ _ _ _ _ _ _ _ _ _ _ _ .

_ _ _ _ _ _ _ _ _ _ _ .

Jesus didn't stay dead! God brought Him back to life again.

You can read about this for yourself in Luke 24 v 1-12.

ONE DAY WONDERS

EASTER EGGSPERIENCE

For Christ died for sins once for all, the righteous for the unrighteous, to bring you to God.

1 Peter 3 v 18a

1. What was surprising about what happened to Jesus? So why was Jesus not surprised?

2. Lots of people let Jesus down that first Easter. When and how do you let God down?

3. Who did Jesus die for and why?

4. What evidence is there that Jesus died and rose again?

5. How does it affect you, knowing Jesus beat even death, is alive again and offers us forgiveness?

EASTER EGGSPERIENCE

When Jesus was arrested, these people all turned their backs on Him. (Take every 2nd letter to see who they are.)

NEELPEIALDAETRESPCRRIOEWSDTESVPEEROYPOL

Start here

¹P _ _ _ _ _   ²P _ _ _ _ _ _ _

³P _ _ _ _ _   ⁴L _ _ _ _ _ _ _

⁵C _ _ _ _

What word is left over?

E _ _ _ _ _ _ _

The people who voted to have Jesus killed weren't the only ones who let Jesus down. The Bible says that **everyone** turns their backs on Jesus. We all let Him down. The Bible calls this sin.

Three days after Jesus died, God brought Him back to life again. Jesus was **alive** – but His **friends** didn't know that yet! Two of them walked to a nearby village, called Emmaus. On the way, **Jesus** came and walked with them – but they didn't **recognise** Him! They were sad and **puzzled** by everything that had happened, so Jesus showed them what the **Scriptures** (the oldest part of the Bible) said about Him.

What do the shaded boxes spell? _ _ _ _ _ _ _

Jesus explained to His friends that He came to rescue His people. You can read this story for yourself in Luke 24 v 13-35.

Drama presentation ideas for older children

GROUP 1:
Palm Sunday and Last Supper
Luke 19 v 28-48; Luke 22 v 1-38

Introduce yourself; then ask if your group have ever seen someone famous in town—what did they and everyone else do or say? Explain that this group is looking at how an important person was welcomed and cheered.

Re-cap on the Palm Sunday story.

Demonstrate how to make palm branches (see below); then each child makes one to use as props in the drama.

Palm branches

Gear
- Thin green card / card stock per child (A4 / US letter)
- Templates for palm leaves (see page 91)
- Newspapers—around eight sheets for each child
- Scissors
- Sellotape (transparent tape)
- Felt-tip pens

1. Take eight sheets of newspaper and roll up along the longest side so you have a long stem. Fasten tape several times around the stem.

2. Place the leaf template on the green card and draw round it.

3. Copy the cutting lines from the template onto the green paper.

4. Cut round the green leaf, and cut along the lines so that your leaf is in seven parts. Assemble these on the floor in front of you in the shape of the leaf.

5. Take the top section of the leaf and tape it to the top of your newspaper stem so that it sticks out beyond the newspaper.

6. Take the next section of the leaf, and place it below the top one, leaving a 1cm gap—about the width of a child's finger. Tape it to the newspaper stem.

7. Continue with the remaining sections of leaves in order, leaving a small gap between each section.

8. If children finish early, get them to decorate their palm branches with the word "Hosanna!" or anything else that they might shout to Jesus.

Chat about their favourite food and memorable meals.

Re-cap the last supper—quickly run through the bread and wine and why Christians still take communion today.

Then as a group, practise acting out the two passages (eg: by miming or saying simple phrases as the story is read out from the Bible passage).

GROUP 2:
Arrest and denial
Luke 22 v 39-71

Introduce yourself; then ask if your group have ever been let down by friends and how it made them feel. Encourage them to strike a pose to show you!

Go over what Peter had to say about the arrest and denial of Jesus.

Demonstrate how to make swords (see below); then each child makes one.

Swords

Gear
- Cardboard boxes or thick card / card stock
- Felt-tip pens
- Masking tape or duct tape
- Sellotape (transparent tape)
- Kitchen foil
- Sword templates (see page 91)
- Scissors and knife for cutting cardboard
- Glue stick (optional—for securing down the foil and for decorations)
- A variety of thin sticks or tubes to use one in the centre of your cardboard sword to give it strength.

1. Draw two outlines of a sword on the card and cut out.

2. Tape your stick or tube in the centre of the sword. Make sure a lot of it is in the handle (for strength).

3. Put the second sword outline on top and tape the two halves together.

4. Now wrap the sword blade in foil—making sure the shiny side is showing.

5. Add details and decorations to the sword.

Then as a group, practise acting out the passage (eg: by miming or saying simple phrases as the story is read out from the Bible passage).

ONE DAY WONDERS

GROUP 3:
Trial and crucifixion
Luke 23

Introduce yourself; then ask if your group have ever been blamed for something they didn't do, eg: eat the last bit of cake or break a model in the classroom. Talk about how you might feel and what you would do.

Then ask them to think about a time they deserved to be in trouble—and how they would have felt if someone took their punishment.

Go over what Barabbas had to say.

Demonstrate how to make a salt-dough crown of thorns or a nail cross (see below); then each child makes one.

Crown of thorns

Gear
- 4 cups of plain flour
- 2 cups of table salt
- 2 cups of water
- Toothpicks

1. Mix flour and salt.

2. Mix with enough water to make a stiff clay.

3. Knead until smooth to remove any air bubbles.

4. Roll three long ropes and loosely plait them. Form plait into a circle and stick toothpicks throughout the entire crown.

5. Bake at 160° F for an hour or until it is dry and light brown.

Nail crosses

Gear
- Two long masonry nails per child
- Two medium masonry nails per child
- Thin wire

1. Place the two long nails side by side, facing opposite directions.

2. Wind wire round the two nails several times, near each end.

3. Do the same for the medium nails.

4. Place the medium nails across the long ones to make a cross. Wind wire round diagonally both ways until firm.

5. Bring the wire up to the top and wind round the head.

6. Make a hanging loop and wind wire round the head several times again.

Then as a group, practise acting out the passage (eg: by miming or saying simple phrases as the story is read out from the Bible passage).

STEP 2   STEP 4   STEP 6

GROUP 4:
Resurrection
Luke 24

Introduce yourself; then show the group a bulb and ask if they have ever planted bulbs. What did the bulbs grow into? What do they think this bulb will grow into? It looks dry and dead, but if you plant it something amazing happens—show them a flower.

Explain that later we're going to see how Jesus actually did die but then came back to life—but we're having a sneaky preview…

Go over the passage from Luke (make sure you're familiar with Luke's account yourself).

Demonstrate how to plant the bulb and make the flowers.

Pot of bulbs

Gear
- Plant pots (one per child)
- Soil/compost
- Bulbs
- Paper
- Pencil
- Scissors
- Green pipe cleaners (or straws)
- Tape or glue
- Stapler

1. Fill the pot with enough soil/compost so that bulbs placed on top can then be covered with more soil to bury them at the proper planting depth (at least an inch or more).

2. Put the bulb in and cover with more soil.

3. Trace a child's hand on paper. Cut the tracing out.

4. Curl each of the fingers around a pencil.

5. Using the palm of the handprint, form a cone (with the fingers curling outwards). Glue or tape the cone together to make a flower.

6. Staple the flower to a pipe cleaner or a drinking straw.

7. Draw some leaves on green paper, then cut them out.

8. Staple or tape the leaves to the straw.

9. Make a few of these flowers for a beautiful bouquet.

Then as a group, practise acting out the passage (eg: by miming or saying simple phrases as the story is read out from the Bible passage).

PRESENTATION:
Telling the whole Easter story

In this final session, you will gather all the children together, with parents, and go over the Easter story from Palm Sunday to the Resurrection. Act as the link person drawing out the main points, as the older children act out the different stages. Eg:

- Explain that Jesus wanted to enter the city of Jerusalem in a special way to show that He was the King of the Jews.

- Jesus showed in the last supper that He knew He would be killed shortly.

- Both Judas and Peter let Jesus down, but this was no surprise to Jesus—He knew what would happen because it was all part of God's plan.

- The crowd shouted for Jesus to be crucified and for a criminal called Barabbas to be set free. Pilate did what they had asked.

- Jesus died in our place as well as Barabbas' place. He was taking the punishment we deserve from God so we can be forgiven by Him and be friends with Him for ever. Jesus knew that He would face a horrible death but He was willing to do that because He loves us so much.

- Jesus did not stay dead. Nothing is more powerful than Jesus because He is God. We too can have new life if we believe in Him.

ONE DAY WONDERS

③ LIGHTBUSTERS

JOHN 8 v 12: 9 v 1-41

Aim

To help the children (and their families if it's a family event) to:

▶ know that God is light—He's perfect and we live in darkness and need Him to save us.
▶ understand that Jesus the light of the world can save us and change us.

Memory verse

The Lord is my light and my salvation.
Psalm 27 v 1a (NIV)

Notes for leaders

 Read **John 8 v 12, 9 v 1-41**

Light is a key theme throughout the Bible, as is darkness. Since God is light, and in Him there is no darkness at all (**1 John 1 v 5; 1 Timothy 6 v 16**), it is hardly surprising that the creation account begins with light (**Genesis 1 v 2-5**). Whereas light often relates to God's presence, guidance and salvation (**Exodus 13 v 21-22; Psalm 112 v 4; Psalm 119 v 105; Isaiah 60 v 19-20; 1 Peter 2 v 9**), darkness is linked to separation from God in one form or another (**Exodus 10 v 21-23; Job 17 v 13-16; Isaiah 9 v 2; Matthew 24 v 29-30; Ephesians 5 v 11-14**).

In John 8 v 12, Jesus describes Himself as the "light of the world". This statement is backed up through His life and death, for God sent Jesus into the world, to show us the Father and how we can know Him. Through His birth and through His teachings, Jesus fulfilled Isaiah's prophecies (**Isaiah 9 v 2, 42 v 6; 49 v 6, 9; 51 v 4; 60 v 1-3; Luke 2 v 32; Matthew 4 v 16; John 1 v 4, 5, 9**) as He is the light of revelation—He gives sight to the blind, He works to make God known, He brings belief, He rescues. By believing in Jesus we are able to become the sons of light (**John 12 v 36**) and escape darkness (**John 12 v 46**)—we have life because of His death (**1 John 1 v 7**). Isn't it fantastic to think we can spend eternity in heaven, where there is eternal light (**Colossians 1 v 12; Revelation 21 v 23; 22 v 5**)!

And so we are called to love the light (**John 3 v 20-21**), walk in the light (**1 John 1 v 5-7**), live as children of the light (**Ephesians 5 v 8**), shine like lights (**Matthew 5 v 16**) and expose "fruitless deeds of darkness" (**Ephesians 5 v 11**) to imitate Christ and bring glory to God.

John 9 is a brilliant example of how Jesus as the "light of the world" reveals His identity and gives spiritual sight, thus demanding a response (v 35-41). The miracle at the start of the passage (v 1-7) is another display of His power and divinity. Jesus' answer to the disciples' question (v 2-3) is a helpful reminder that the work of the gospel is God's doing—it is not about what we do or how we package the message. We, like the disciples, need to remember that we have a gracious Saviour, who is at work, for the purpose of His glory.

As the miracle comes under examination, so the blind man's understanding of Jesus develops and his faith grows. He goes from calling Him "the man they call Jesus" (v 11), to "a prophet" (v 17), to saying that Jesus could not be a sinner, for He had shown God-given powers (v 31-32—further recognition of Jesus' identity) and then at the end he believes that Jesus is the Son of Man (v 38) and is saved. The blind man not only grows in understanding, but also obeys Jesus from the beginning when he is sent (v 6), and persists in confessing Jesus, despite the opposition he faces (v 30-34). The reaction of the Jews is in sharp contrast—they refused to believe, despite the evidence. They thought that they knew more than Jesus and they were condemned to judgment (v 28, 39-41). Pray that Jesus would reveal Himself to those you are working with—that they recognise their blindness, regardless of teaching in school or opposition from home. Pray too for boldness as you explain the two sides of the coin: God's judgment and God's mercy, what we need saving from and saving for.

Leader's prayer

 Pray

Father God, thank You that You are light and in You there is no darkness. Thank You that You have revealed Yourself to us through Jesus and we are able to know forgiveness of sins and eternal life. Please help us to live as children of the light and shine as bright beacons for your glory. We pray that You would open the eyes of those we work with. Amen.

Programme Options

In recent years Halloween has become the autumn festival to celebrate, overtaking the traditional English celebration of Bonfire Night in popularity. Although now largely influenced by American television and merchandise in shops, as well as being connected to All Saints Day, some beliefs and practices linked with its pagan roots in Celtic and Roman times have persisted in Halloween.

It is likely that people in your church will hold a range of views about Halloween. While some will see it as innocuous fun, many will want to avoid it or boycott it. One thing is certain: with its focus on fear, death and darkness—and the gospel's focus on hope, eternal life and light—we have another fantastic evangelistic opportunity at this time of year.

See the **Aims** section on page 6 to help you decide who you want to reach out to.

Once you have decided upon your target audience, choose an outline from the three options below. Then select games, crafts, challenges etc (see **Ideas Menu**, pages 72-78) and delegate accordingly.

The tables on the next three pages give you further details about each of the three suggested options for an event at Halloween time. Space is included to add the name of the team member responsible for each activity. You may find it helpful to give copies of this table to each member of your team. You can photocopy this page or download a copy for free from **www.thegoodbook.co.uk/onedaywonders** (see page 3 for further details about downloads).

Option A: Two-hour children's event

15 min	Registration and opening games (begins 10 min before start)
25 min	Together Time 1—songs, team challenges, memory verse, quiz
25 min	Themed crafts (with drinks break)
25 min	Together Time 2—songs, team challenges, Bible story, prayer, quiz
15 min	Small groups
25 min	Themed games

Option B: Four-hour children's event

20 min	Registration and opening activities and challenges (begins 10 min before start)
40 min	Together Time 1—songs, team challenges, memory verse, talk 1, quiz (1st half)
60 min	Rotation 1—games, crafts and small groups
15 min	Half time: "light" refreshments
40 min	Together Time 2—songs, team challenges, prayer, Bible story (talk 2)
60 min	Rotation 2—Drama, banners, bouncy castle or parachute games
15 min	Together Time 3—quiz (2nd half) and prize giving

Option C: One-and-a-half-hour family fun event

10 min	Pumpkin carving and "Who am I?" as families arrive
50 min	Games: Split the entire group into 4 or 6 teams and run a number of games that aim to include everyone and require a mixture of skills.
15 min	Light refreshments and quiz
10 min	Talk
5 mins	Prizes

Option A: Two-hour children's event

Gear

- Name labels and pens
- Registration forms
- Bookmarks and colouring pencils
- Glowsticks
- Materials for your choice of games, challenges and crafts
- Visual aids for the Bible story
- Memory-verse props

- Music and words for songs
- Quiz questions and scoreboard
- Small-group sheets and pencils for each child
- Prizes
- Refreshments
- Publicity for regular services and children's groups plus any upcoming events

Time	Activity	✔	Leader
	Tick when materials are ready for each activity		
Before event	Preparation eg: decorate the room, get crafts ready, etc		
One hour before	Team meeting for prayer and final instructions		
10 minutes before (for 15 minutes)	Children arrive, register and are given a name label—before being taken to their opening activities eg: bookmark colouring, glowstick jewellery, opening games (see **Ideas Menu** for Light games, pages 76-78)		
25 minutes Together Time 1	Welcome—introduction of leaders, what's going to happen, rules etc Team challenge (see **Ideas Menu**, page 72) Song (see **Music Spot**, page 72 for song suggestions) Team challenge Memory verse (see **Ideas Menu**, page 73) Song Quiz (see **Ideas Menu**, page 73)		
25 minutes	Crafts (see **Ideas Menu**, pages 73-75) Drink and a snack in groups		
25 minutes Together Time 2	Team challenges Song Bible story (**Talk idea 1**, page 68) Song Prayer (see **Ideas Menu**, page 75) Quiz		
15 minutes	Small-groups time (see **Ideas Menu**, page 75)		
25 minutes	Games (see **Ideas Menu**, pages 76-78)—maybe do one big game all together at the end. Promote upcoming events and award any prizes.		

Option B: Four-hour children's event

4 *Light Fun*

Gear

- Registration forms, name labels and pens
- Bookmarks and colouring pencils
- Glowsticks
- Materials for your games, challenges and crafts
- Visual aids for the Eyewitness accounts
- Memory-verse props
- Small-groups sheets and pencil for each child

- Music and words for songs
- Quiz questions and scoreboard
- Refreshments
- Copies of play scripts
- Publicity for regular services and children's groups plus any upcoming events

Time	Activity	✔	Leader
	Tick when materials are ready for each activity	✔	
Before event	Preparation eg: decorate room, get crafts ready etc		
One hour before	Team meeting for prayer and final instructions		
10 minutes before (for 20 minutes)	Children arrive, register and are given a name label—before being taken to their opening activities eg: bookmark colouring, glowstick jewellery, opening games (see **Ideas Menu** for Light games, pages 76-78)		
40 minutes Together Time 1	Welcome—introduction of leaders, what's going to happen, rules etc Team challenge (see **Ideas Menu**, page 72) Song (see **Music Spot**, page 72) Team challenge Song Talk 1 (see page 68) Quiz (1st half, see **Ideas Menu**, page 73)		
60 minutes Rotation 1 (20 mins on each)	Split the children into three age-groups and rotate them around the three activities, spending 20 minutes on each: Activity 1—Sports (see **Ideas Menu**, pages 76-78) Activity 2—Crafts (see **Ideas Menu**, pages 73-75) Activity 3—Small groups (see **Ideas Menu**, page 75)		
15 minutes	Half-time break: During this time serve "light refreshments" eg: drinks and snacks If your half-time break is over lunchtime, you may provide something simple eg: hot dogs, crisps/chips, biscuits/cookies, fruit; alternatively, your publicity could mention bringing sandwiches.		
40 minutes Together Time 2	Team challenge (see **Ideas Menu**, page 72) Song Prayer Team challenge Bible story (Talk 2—see page 69) Song		
60 minutes Rotation 2 (20 mins on each)	Split the children back into three age-groups and rotate them around the three activities, spending 20 minutes on each: Activity 1—Drama (see **Ideas Menu**, page 76) Activity 2—Team banners (see **Ideas Menu**, page 73) Activity 3—Bouncy castle or parachute games (see **Ideas Menu**, page 76)		
15 minutes	Quiz (2nd half, see **Ideas Menu**, page 73) Prize giving Announcements for other upcoming events		

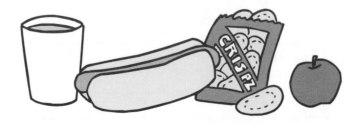

Option C: One-and-a-half-hour family fun event

Gear

- Materials for your choice of games, challenges and crafts
- Visual aids for the talk
- Wall quiz
- Quiz questions and scoreboard

- Refreshments
- Prizes
- Publicity for Easter services or events

Time	Activity	✔	Leader
	Tick when materials are ready for each activity		
Before event	Preparation eg: decorate room, get games and refreshments ready etc		
One hour before	Team meeting for prayer and final instructions		
10 minutes before (for 15 minutes)	Doors open Pumpkin carving challenge (see **Ideas Menu**, page 75) "Who am I?" icebreaker game (see **Ideas Menu**, page 78)		
8 minutes	Introduction; then play "Lightbusters" (see **Ideas Menu**, page 77) as one large group.		
2 minutes	Split entire group into 4 or 6 teams. All teams will compete in each game at the same time. Try to choose a variety of games that will include everyone and need a range of skills.		
40 minutes	Family teams rotate around the different light-themed activities.		
15 minutes	"Light" refreshments Quiz (see **Ideas Menu**, page 73)		
10 minutes	Bible talk (Talk idea 1, page 68)		
5 minutes	Prizes and announcements		

Talk idea 1

Suitable for children or family events

You will need to prepare the following props as well as reading the talk through and practising with the candle several times so that you are familiar with it.

Gear

▶ Matches
▶ A "magic candle" (the kind that relights itself)

Bible talk

Let's start with a quick-fire game. I'm going to say a word and I want you to say the opposite of it. Ready…?

• **Sad** (happy)
• **Up** (down)
• **Left** (right)
• **Wet** (dry)
• **Hard** (soft)
• **Frown** (smile)
• **Top** (bottom)
• **Alive** (dead)
• **Young** (old)
• **Big** (little)
• **Rich** (poor)
• **Wide** (narrow)
• **Good** (bad)
• **Light** (dark)

Well done! Well, we're going to be thinking a little about light and dark now.

Do you know what? Jesus once said He was the "light of the world"! He was the original "lightbuster"! You see light in the Bible always means good and dark means bad. And you know and I know that light will always be more powerful than dark. Think about when you walk into a dark room and turn on the switch—dark's defeated every time.

So when Jesus said "I am the light of the world", He was showing that He's good and He's powerful. And not only that, light helps us—it shows us what's really there and guides us. Jesus was saying He had come to show people how they could follow God and have eternal life. So let's have a think why Jesus would say that and what He came to show us.

Just close your eyes for a minute. I know it's probably not very dark, but in the very beginning of time everything was totally dark, pitch black, not a flicker in sight. Can you imagine that? No light whatsoever. But it didn't stay like that. Instead when God, who's always been around, started creating things, the very first thing He said was, "Let there be light"—and there was—the total opposite.

Candle: Light your magic candle.

Open your eyes. Isn't that incredible? Just being able to speak and things appear—out of nowhere. How powerful is that?! And God didn't stop there, He kept on creating; kept on speaking and things kept appearing; kept on showing His power and His wisdom. Sky and sea, plants and animals, fish and birds, sun, moons and stars. Beautiful, amazing, colourful things—things which we need because God loves us and wants to provide for us, and things that were all absolutely perfect too, 100% good. Perfect and good because God Himself is perfect and good, as well as powerful, loving and everlasting. God is light and He was pleased with what He made.

But do you know what? It didn't stay perfect for long. It was like the light was put out.

Candle: Blow out candle.

First Adam and Eve ignored God and disobeyed His rule about eating from a tree. They thought they knew better than God—and they're not the only ones, that was just the start. People disobeyed God, they said wrong things, did wrong things and thought wrong things. Even though God is good, perfect and powerful, they stopped caring about Him and even thinking about Him. And the world became full of more and more darkness, lying and stealing, fighting and illness, jealousy and pain. But even though there's all this wrong, God is still here.

Candle: The candle should have relit itself.

Nothing can get rid of God, nothing can beat Him. He's still powerful and perfect, still everlasting and loving.

However God doesn't like it when we lie to our mums, or hit our brother, or forget to talk to God. These things don't just make God sad, but also cross. In fact, we deserve to be punished for the wrong things we do.

Candle: Blow out candle.

Dark and light don't mix, do they? You either have one or the other. They are separated—and we deserve to be separated from God, the light. Our punishment is not to be His friend, not to be with Him in heaven. To be cut off from all good things and from God. But God doesn't want that, He wants us to live in the light again.

And so He sent a gift. A present for us.

Candle: Candle should have relit itself.

A bright crowd of angels that made the sky light told the shepherds about the gift. Wise men followed a bright light or a star to find out more about the gift. What was the gift? (Jesus) Yes, God sent Jesus to bring light to the world. He sent Jesus to live a perfect life and to teach us about the right way to live—in the light, following Him. He also sent Jesus to do amazing, powerful things like calming a storm, feeding 5000 people with a bit of bread and fish, turning water into wine, and bringing hope and light to people's lives by making people better. Jesus could do all this because this gift was God in skin. He was light!

But do you know what? Some people didn't like the fact that Jesus was from God. They didn't like the fact His light showed up areas they needed to clean up and change in their lives. So they decided to get rid of the light. They decided to kill Jesus. When Jesus was 33, they had Him arrested, beaten, bullied, nailed to a cross and left to die. And as He hung there in the middle of the day, it went dark.

Candle: Blow out candle.

Dark seemed to beat light. It was like the nasty people had won. Jesus was dead. But do you know why it went dark in the day? It was all part of God's plan for Jesus the light. It went dark as Jesus died in our place, as Jesus took the punishment we deserve on Himself. He was cut off and separated from God, from light, from all things good so we could be forgiven.

But that wasn't the only part of God's plan. Jesus' light will never go out. Nothing can beat God as He's all-powerful and everlasting.

Candle: Candle should have relit itself.

And so three days later Jesus rose from the dead. He came alive again, proving that He is God and that we can live in the light, we can be His friends and we can go to heaven. We don't have to be in the dark. We have a choice.

We can keep going as we are, doing our own thing, doing wrong things, and so live in the dark—for ever. Or we can say sorry to God for the wrong things we've done and ask Him to forgive us. We can thank Jesus for dying in our place and we can ask Him to help change us. If we do that, we know that we have a place in heaven and God's help to shine for Him.

You see, if someone gives you a gift, you want to show you're thankful. God wants us to show we're thankful for Jesus by being mini-lights for Him, being lightbusters, by being like Him in caring for others and living the right way—doing what God wants, light things that show other people what God's like and helping them want to move from dark to light. What choice will you make? Will you ask Jesus, the light of the world, to rescue you?

Talk idea 2
Suitable for children's events

You will need to collect the following things as well as reading the drama through several times so that you are familiar with it. The drama is based on John 9, so read through the Bible passage several times as well.

Gear
▶ Enough copies of the script (pages 69-71) for each person taking part
▶ Props and costumes if required
▶ Blindfolds (scarves or airline sleep masks)
▶ Banana

To begin with all four witnesses will be blindfolded (except the blind man) and asked to identify a banana in front of them. This will hopefully show how our attitudes can get in the way of us seeing the truth. Then the interview will start.

Drama

Newsreader: Hello and welcome to Lightbusters News 24, live here from the studio.

Today's toptastic topic is all about what stops us seeing the truth. Coming up shortly, we have the latest exclusive on Jesus. In recent weeks we've heard how He turned water into wine, fed 5000 people and stopped a storm—and this time He's only gone and healed a blind man.

But first in the studio we have a demonstration of how we too can be blinded. As you can see, with me today are four people, who are all going to be set the same task. They have to identify the item placed in front of them. The trouble is some of them can't see. So let's ask the first person—let's just call him Mr Proud—what this item is.

Pharisee: You mean I have to feel the item and tell you what it is? You must be joking, there's no way I'm going to do that! Don't you know who I am? I'm far too important to be playing silly games.

Newsreader: Ah, it seems our first guest is too proud to work out what the object is. He thinks he's too important, and that what he thinks matters the most. Let's try our second volunteer, who we'll call Miss Puzzle. Can you work out what this item is?

Neighbour: Sorry, I'm a little unsure what I'm meant to do. Do I feel the object, or smell it or what? I don't really know what's going on, it's a bit confusing...

Newsreader: So it seems our second guest is too confused to work out what the object is. She doesn't understand, and, in a way, being puzzled is blinding her to the truth. Well, let's move on to our next guest, Mrs Scared, and ask her to tell us what this mystery item is.

Mother: Ooh I don't like this, just putting my hands out, I mean, it could be anything, couldn't it? No thanks, I'd rather not, it's just a little too scary for me, thanks anyway.

Newsreader: Oh dear, we're not doing too well. It seems this lady is too scared to work out what the object is. Everyone so far has been blinded by different things—pride, puzzlement, and now fear! Well, let's try our last volunteer. Could you tell us what this object is please?

Blind man: Why, it's a banana! I can see that quite clearly.

Newsreader: At last, someone who can see the truth! And not just anyone—you're the blind man, aren't you?

Blind man: Yeah, that's right.

Newsreader: Amazing! How incredible! Well let's get to the bottom of this extraordinary story. All our guests here in the studio were actually involved in Jesus' latest miracle, so if they would please remove their blindfolds, let's find out exactly what happened. I wonder, even with their blindfolds off, if they're still blind to the truth? Let's start with Miss Puzzle shall we? How did this extraordinary story begin?

Neighbour: Ooh well, I could hardly believe my eyes, I tell you! I'm a neighbour of this blind man—well, he's not blind anymore is he, that's the point! Anyway, I saw this man who used to be blind walking around, and I said to my friend, "Isn't that the man who used to be blind and beg on the streets?" And she said she didn't think so, it was just someone who looked the same. And then the blind man who wasn't blind anymore came up to me and my friend and said that yes, it was him!

Newsreader: And what happened then?

Neighbour: Well, I asked him how his eyes were opened, how he could see—and he said the guy they call Jesus had passed him, and Jesus had said that he was the light of the world, or something like that. Then Jesus had made some mud and put it on the blind man's eyes. Jesus then told him to wash in the pool of Siloam, and when he washed he could suddenly see! It was amazing, but a bit puzzling: how was Jesus so powerful? So I asked him where Jesus was, and he said he didn't know, so me and the other neighbours took him to see the Pharisees, you know, the religious leaders.

Newsreader: Thank you. Well it seems this lady is too puzzled to understand what was happening or who Jesus is, just like she was too puzzled to reach out and work out what the object was. I hope you're not like that. Do you know who Jesus is and why He was so powerful? His miracles show us He's God.

Well, let's find out what happened next. Hello sir, thank you for coming on Lightbusters News 24. Am I right in saying that you're the religious leader these ladies brought the man who used to be blind to?

Pharisee: Yes, I am, and they were right to bring the man to me—after all, I am rather important. The story is shocking, absolutely shocking! The blind man, if he was really blind, said that Jesus made him able to see! But if that's true, Jesus made him better on the Sabbath, our special day to worship God, and personally, I think that's awful. The man said he thought Jesus was a messenger from God, but I don't see how Jesus can be if He was breaking our rules like that.

Newsreader: So you don't think Jesus healed him?

Pharisee: That's hardly the issue. What matters is who Jesus is!

Newsreader: You don't think He's from God?

Pharisee: Certainly not! It was clear this blind man was a follower of Jesus, but I AM MOST DEFINITELY NOT. I refuse to believe there's anything special about a man who breaks my rules like that! I know better than Jesus!

Newsreader: Er, thank you. Well, if the neighbour was too puzzled to see the truth, that Pharisee is too proud! He thought he was too important to work out the banana at the beginning, and it seems he thinks He's better than Jesus! I wonder, do you believe in Jesus? Do you believe all He taught and did is true?

Well, so far we know that Jesus has healed the blind man, but that the neighbours didn't understand how, and that the leaders didn't want to understand. Well, let's go now to the mother of the blind man, and find out what happened. Madam, could you confirm that your son has been blind since he was born?

Mother: That's just what that religious leader asked me! Yes, that man is my son, and yes, he's always been blind. Then the leaders asked me and my husband how it was that my son could see again.

Newsreader: And what did you say?

Mother: Well, my son is grown-up now, so my husband and I told them to ask him, seeing as he's old enough to speak for himself. To be honest, I was a bit scared of what those leaders would think if I talked about Jesus, so I just told them to ask my son about it. I'd heard they'd chuck us out of certain places for talking about Jesus. And I was right to keep my mouth shut too, because when my son talked about Jesus, the leaders threw him out!

Newsreader: Oh dear, so the neighbour was too puzzled to see who Jesus was, the leaders were too proud, and the man's mum was too scared, just like she was too scared to work out what the object was. Well, let's finally understand this story, and talk to the man that it's all about.

Blind man: Actually, the story's all about Jesus, and who He is. It's not really about me.

Newsreader: And who do you think He is?

Blind man: Well, at first I thought He was a messenger from God, because only someone from God could do such amazing and kind things. But after the religious leaders threw me out, Jesus came and found me. He asked me if I believed in the Son of Man. That's a name for the Rescuer God had promised the world. I asked Jesus: "Who is he, so that I can believe in him?" And Jesus said that He Himself was the Son of Man—He was God and had come to rescue us! And I put my trust in Him. I'm going to follow Him and try to live in a way that pleases Him.

Newsreader: Wow! So Jesus is the promised Rescuer from God?! Amazing. All those other people couldn't see it, because they were too puzzled, or proud, or scared, but this man, who used to be blind, believed it and put his trust in Jesus! Incredible! So what did Jesus say then?

Blind man: He said that He'd come to the world to show people the truth about God and how they could be friends with Him—but He also said He would punish people who didn't believe He was God and didn't believe they needed to ask God to forgive them.

Newsreader: OK—so you were blind, but Jesus helped you see—not just see trees and stars and people, but also see who He is—God's Son, our Rescuer. I guess that's what Jesus meant when He said He was the light of the world, that He had come to help people see the truth, just like light helps us see things.

So what about you? Do you understand who Jesus is, and do you want to follow Him too? Are you going to admit you need His help and rescue? Will you ask Him to forgive you and thank Him for dying in your place, taking your punishment? It can be hard at times living in a way that pleases God but don't be scared—He helps you and changes you.

Well, that's the end of today's news. Thank you for watching. Goodbye.

IDEAS MENU

Team challenges

These can be used to create team spirit and an enthusiastic environment. If you have divided the children into teams, it's good to get a representative up from each one. They are useful for your opening activities as the children arrive at the event.

Apple-bobbing team challenge

Gear
- Washing-up bowl
- Water
- Apples (lots)

The total number of apples bobbed within the allotted time will be recorded, points being awarded for the number of apples bobbed. Keep a record of the best.

Pin-the-flame-on-the-candle team challenge

Gear
- Candle poster (see page 92)
- Flame (see page 92)
- Scarf

Just like "Pin the Tail on the Donkey" except this uses a poster of a candle. Blindfold the players one at a time while they take turns trying to get the closest to the proper location for the flame. Keep a record of the best.

Monster-builder team challenge

Gear
- Boxes
- Other "junk" (eg: cardboard tubes, plastic bottles, foil containers)

Children in a set time limit build as tall a box monster as possible—points awarded for height and creativity in design. Keep a record of the best.

Smarties-in-a-jar team challenge

Gear
- Smarties or m&m's
- Jar

Prepare a small glass jar filled with smarties. Let the children guess the numbers. Keep a record of estimates.

Bust-a-gut team challenge

Gear
- Tins
- Balls

Set up a "tin can alley"—a chance to throw a ball at the cans and see how many they can knock down. Keep a record of the best.

Coin-it team challenge

Gear
- Washing-up bowl (or bucket)
- Water
- Coins
- Targets (eg: black metal shapes, or targets drawn on the bowl with permanent marker pen)

A washing-up bowl with black targets in the bottom of it is filled with water. Children try to drop shiny coins onto the black, to cover dark with light. Keep a record of the best.

Blindfolded-champions team challenge

Gear
- Blindfolds (eg: scarves or airline sleep masks)
- Balls
- Oranges
- Paper and pens

A volunteer from each team is blindfolded and takes a challenge, eg: draw a picture of an elephant, peel an orange, dribble a ball. If you choose two from each team, you could have a blindfolded feeding race—one person sits down and their blindfolded partner stands in front of them (facing). Those blindfolded have to feed their partners chocolate mousse/pudding or baby food. Those seated can direct but not touch. Points are awarded for speed and tidiness.

Music spot

Choose from the following song suggestions for the various song slots.

How cool is that! (track 4) of Johnny Burns' *How cool is that!* CD

God is a holy God (track 10) of *The King, the snake and the promise* CD

Clap your hands (track 1) of *The King, the snake and the promise* CD

I'm following the King (track 1) of the *Meet the King* CD

My King (track 12) of the *Earth Movers* CD

The Saviour of the World (track 16) of the *Promises, promises* CD

Memory verse

**The Lord is my light and my salvation.
Psalm 27 v 1a**

Gear
▶ A torch/flashlight

Show the torch (switched off). Explain that when it's off, it's not doing what it's made to do, but when it's on, it lights up the darkness, it guides us and helps us. Explain that Jesus described Himself as a light as He is 100% good and He shows us God and how we should live. He guides us and helps us.

Now teach the verse with the following actions:
The Lord (point up) **is my** (point to self) **light** (twinkling fingers) **and my** (point to self) **salvation** (action hero pose). **Psalm 27 v 1a**

After saying it a few times, explain that they are going to do it in teams. They have to watch you carefully so that when you point the torch at them, they say the next part, eg: **The Lord / is my light / and my / salvation / Psalm 27 / verse 1a**.

Beyond the stars quiz

Gear
▶ Card / card stock stars with different amounts of points written on the back of most, but some with pictures of meteors

Arrange the stars, either on the wall or on a board, in rows of 6, so the points and meteors can't be seen. Each row should have stars with a mixture of points, and a meteor.

This quiz is based on the game "Play your cards right". When a child answers a question correctly, turn over a star and let the team see how many points they have scored. The team can either decide to "stick" and keep the points or "risk" and try to gain more. They can keep trying to turn over more points but if they get a meteor, they lose all the points from that go.

Use the quiz to reinforce what has been taught in a fun way and to help teams score points. Make sure the questions are clear and pitched at all ages.

Group banner

Gear
▶ Large sheets of black paper (probably 4 or 5 for small groups to work on)— 70 cm x 1m, with "light" written on it in big lettering and bricks drawn on, like a wall
▶ Lots of shiny/coloured paper
▶ Scissors
▶ Glue
▶ Paint and paintbrushes
▶ Stickers
▶ Water sprayers filled with watered-down paint

1. The youngest children can cut small pieces of shiny and coloured paper, and stick them onto the lettering.

2. Slightly older children can paint all sorts of decorations over the wall eg: swirls, stars. In addition they could decorate with stickers and squirt the diluted paint over it, with the sprayers.

3. The oldest children are to "graffiti" write all over the wall—putting on it words they think of when they hear the word "light" and the word "Jesus".

NB. This craft will take a while and is one which is good for different ages to work on at different stages of their rotational activities.

Paper lanterns

Gear
▶ Paper (A4 / US letter)
▶ Stapler or glue
▶ Scissors
▶ Felt-tip pens
▶ Stickers

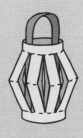

1. Children to decorate a piece of A4 / US letter paper with dots, swirls, stars etc.

2. Fold the paper in half horizontally.

3. Make a series of cuts in the paper about 1-2cm apart, cutting from the folded edge to about 2cm from the other edge of the paper.

4. Unfold the paper and roll it into a tube.

5. Staple or stick the edges together.

6. Then give the children a strip of paper to attach to the top to make a handle.

Lighthouse

Craft

Gear
- Large sheets to protect work surface and aprons for children (eg: old shirts worn backwards)
- White card / card stock
- Plastic cups—with their bases cut off in advance
- Small plastic pots (eg: from mini fromage frais or yogurt)
- Paper plates
- Pebbles
- Paints
- Grey acrylic paint
- Paint brushes
- Sellotape
- Yellow stickers / yellow paper

1. Children paint their plates blue.

2. Then paint the cup grey.

3. Next roll the card into a narrow cone shape (so one end fits into the plastic cup and the other into the fromage frais pot). Stick the cone together and paint red horizontal stripes round it.

4. Stick yellow paper around the fromage frais pot.

5. Assemble the model by putting the cup upside down on the plate; then stick the card cone through it. Pop the yellow fromage frais pot on the top.

6. Finally scatter pebbles around the blue plate.

Glass candle-holders

Craft

Gear
- Low-cost glass candle-holders
- Glass pens or paints
- Tea-lights

Children to decorate the candle holders.

Glowstick jewellery

Craft

Gear
- Glowsticks
- Connectors

Children could just make a band bangle or necklace. Alternatively they could try plaiting the glowsticks or twist two together.

Light jars

Craft

Gear
- Jars (eg: from baby food)
- Vegetable oil
- Food colouring
- Shells
- Glitter
- Beads
- Glass pens

1. Let each of the children fill one of the jars halfway with water and add two or three drops of food colouring.

2. Add shells, beads and glitter.

3. Fill each child's jar to the top with the oil.

4. Screw the lid on tightly.

5. Decorate the outside of the jar with glass pens.

6. Let the children shake their wave jars back and forth to create waves.

Bookmarks

Craft

Gear
- Card bookmarks with space and sunny scenes (templates on page 94)
- Scissors
- Glue
- Felt-tip pens
- String/wool
- Hole punch
- Laminator and laminating pouches

1. Children to choose and cut out a bookmark; then colour it.

2. A leader then laminates the bookmark.

3. Punch a hole at one end.

4. Tie string/wool through as a tassel.

Biscuit decorating

Cooking

Gear
- Plain (eg: Rich tea) biscuits/cookies
- Tubes of coloured icing
- Sweets and other decorations

1. Decorate biscuits with happy faces, stars or candles.

2. Eat and enjoy!

Craft
Star mobiles

Gear
- Wire coathangers
- Yellow ribbon
- Gold card / card stock
- Star template (see page 93)
- Scissors
- Hole punch
- Glitter
- Glue

1. Draw round the star template 4 or 5 times on gold card.

2. Cut out the stars.

3. Put glue on the stars and sprinkle with glitter.

4. Hole punch the top of each star.

5. Cut different lengths of ribbon and thread through the star.

6. Tie to the coathanger.

Craft
Stained-glass windows

Gear
- Overhead transparencies with pictures printed on
- OHT permanent pens or glass pens

Before the event, photocopy the templates on pages 94-95 onto photocopiable overhead transparencies. Children can colour in the pictures using permanent OHT (overhead transparency) pens and/or glass pens.

Craft
Pumpkin carving

Gear
- Pumpkins
- Paper
- Marker pens
- Knife
- Ice-cream scoop
- Bowl

This is best done in small groups (or families) and can be a competition. Each group must have an adult for the carving.

1. Draw a circle or hexagon around the stalk of the pumpkin to make the lid; then cut it out.

2. Remove all the seeds from the lid.

3. Draw a design on paper; then copy it onto the pumpkin with a marker pen.

4. Carefully cut around the lines to make the face and push out the eyes, nose and mouth.

5. Scoop out the pulp, seeds and flesh.

Teach us to pray
Prayer Suggestion

Gear
- Large sheet of black card / card stock
- Three card circles: one red with "no" written on the back, one orange with "wait" written on the back, and one green with "yes" written on the back. Stick these circles on the card with Blu-Tack reuseable adhesive, assembled like a traffic light.

Check the children understand what prayer is. Explain that it is talking with God, and is something we can do anytime, anywhere, about anything. Tell them how God loves us to talk with Him, and He not only listens but always answers. Because God loves us so much and knows us inside out, He knows what is best for us and will always answer in the best way, giving us what we need. In fact, the way God answers is a bit like traffic lights…

Ask the children what the green light stands for (go). Turn the green circle round and explain that sometimes God says "yes".

Then ask them what the amber light stands for (get ready or wait). Turn around the orange circle and explain that sometimes God says "wait" or "not yet".

Finally ask what the red light stands for (stop). Turn around the red circle and explain that sometimes God says "no", when what we've asked for is not the best thing for us.

Then pray with the children:

Father God, thank You that we can speak to You anytime, anywhere, about anything. Thank You that You always hear us and answer. Thank You that You give us what we need and You want the best for us. Please help us to know You more, to trust You more and to live Your way. Amen.

Small groups
Small groups

Options A and B both include time for the children to be split into small groups where they can think about the teaching they have heard.

Pages 81-83 include copies of fun sheets to use in these groups. The sheets have been designed for three age groups: 4-7s (Reception to Year 2)—page 81, 7-9s (Years 3-4)—page 82, 9-11s (Years 5-6)—page 83. With the older groups, you may also choose to have Bibles available so that they can read for themselves some of the Bible story they have heard. If you don't have

sufficient Bibles available, you can copy the relevant text from www.biblegateway.com to print your own sheets.

On pages 79-80 there are notes to help the leaders of the small groups. Please give copies of these to each small group leader in advance, so that they can prepare thoroughly. This is particularly important if the small groups are being led by an inexperienced leader or helper (which may be the case if you have a small team and a large number of children).

Drama suggestion

Briefly recap the story. Split the children into smaller groups and give them each a section of the John 9 story, eg:

- Jesus healing the man.

- The puzzled neighbours questioning the man.

- The proud Pharisees chatting to the man.

- The Pharisees talking to the scared parents.

- Jesus meeting the man who can now see and who kneels and worships Jesus.

Each small group has to work on acting out their part of the story. Depending on the age of the group, you may want to narrate it while they act, or you may want to get them to put together a freeze frame (like photo shots or tableaux).

Put a mini-performance together where they each show the other small groups. Afterwards discuss with them how the different people felt and how they saw Jesus. Then ask the children what they think about Jesus.

Parachute games

Mushroom
Children stand around the parachute holding the edges. After you have counted to three, shout "Mushroom" and all the children raise the parachute. Call out a colour or other feature of clothing, or favourite football team, or age etc. Those children swap places by running under the parachute while it is in the air, before it drops back down again.

Cat and mouse
One player (the cat) is on top of the parachute and another (the mouse) is underneath. Everyone else creates a choppy "sea" with the parachute by shaking it up and down. The cat tries to catch the mouse. Once the mouse has been caught, swap over with new players.

Shark
One player is selected as the "shark" and everyone else sits on the floor with their feet under the chute. The shark captures the feet of other players, who get pulled under the parachute with a scream, and themselves become more sharks. Have a couple of leaders stood on the outside as lifeguards—when they hear the children scream, they have to try and race round and rescue the child before they are dragged under.

GOAL!
Split the children around the parachute into two teams. Each team has to try and shake a ball off the opponents' half of the parachute. They are only allowed to shake the parachute and head the ball.

Light on your feet

Gear
- Paper (white or a bright colour)
- CD
- CD player

Play this like "musical chairs", but use pieces of paper in place of the chairs. Children must walk around the paper until you turn off the music, at which point they must stand inside one of the "bright lights" or they're out. Every few minutes, take away a bit of paper, until only one remains.

Light fight

Gear
- Balloons (40 plus a few spares in case some pop)
- Chairs

Split children into four teams and divide the room into four quarters using chairs. Each team has 10 balloons. The children hit the balloons from their own quarter to the others. After 20 or 30 seconds of this, the leader shouts out "3... 2... 1... zero". Whichever team has the most balloons on "zero" loses a life. All four teams start with three lives. When a team have no lives left, they sit down. From then on, the other teams lose a life if they knock a balloon into the area where a dead team is. The winner is the team with lives left when the rest have none.

Solar-system scrap

Gear
▶ Ball

Divide into boys (Aliens) at one end of the hall, and girls (Astronauts) at other end. A leader shouts out: "Aliens": Boys run to the opposite end and back again. "Astronauts": Girls run to the opposite end and back again. "Battle in the solar system": Both run to the opposite end and back. While they are running, the leaders attempt to "knock them out of the sky" by hitting them below the knee with a small, soft ball. Those knocked out of the sky sit out until only one person is left.

Relay races

Gear
▶ Balloons / bean bags / balls / straws / rice crispies (depending on type of race)

Split children into 2, 3 or 4 groups; then line them up in the room. If the children are numbered, they can compete individually by running to the front wall, back wall and back to seat. Variations can be made such as "moon walk with a planet" (balloon between knees), "asteroid jumping" (hopping) etc. Alternatively the children can compete as a team, eg: "passing the planet" (balloon between knees or beanbag / tennis ball under chin) or "shooting stars" (pass rice crispies along the line, using straws).

Escape ball

Gear
▶ A ball

Form a circle (galaxy) with legs apart and feet touching. One child in the middle attempts to hit a ball (star), with their hand only, through the legs of those in the circle. Those in the circle can only use their hands to stop the ball. If the ball goes out of the circle between someone's legs, that child swaps places with the person in the middle.

Lightbusters

Gear
▶ Balloons
▶ String, wool or curling ribbon

Give each child a balloon and attach the balloon around each child's ankle with string, wool or curling ribbon. At the sound of "**Go**", each child will try to pop the other children's balloons without having his/hers popped. The one left with the unpopped balloon wins.

Alternatively, if you are playing this at a family fun event, children could climb on their parent's back and hold the balloon. They have to try and knock another child's balloon out of their hand and pop it.

Make sure the playing space gets smaller as the number of players reduces.

Stuck on the moon

One or more players can be "it". This is a game of "tag" and when a child is tagged, they stand with their legs apart. They are set free when someone crawls under their legs. The game is over when everyone has been tagged.

Light-fingered!

Gear
▶ 9 beanbags
▶ 4 chairs

Split the children into 4 groups, one in each corner of the room. In the teams number the children 1,2,3,4,5... Have a chair for each team set up in a square, at an equal distance from each other. Put nine beanbags in the middle of the floor. Shout a number. Number "X" from each team must collect the beanbags (one at a time) from the middle and put them on their team chair. Then they need to steal beanbags from the other chairs. The winner is the first to get three on their chair.

Additional rules are:

1. Only carry one beanbag at a time.

2. Beanbags cannot be thrown—they must be placed on the chair.

3. You cannot interfere with or stop someone stealing a beanbag.

Comets and flying saucers

Gear
▶ Small flexi cones (the kind used as markers for games)

Place enough flexi cones on the floor so that there is at least one for each child. Half of them need to be placed on the floor in the normal way, and half upside down. This creates the comets and flying saucers.

Divide the children into two groups. Depending on whether they are a comet or flying saucer, they have to turn the flexi cones over for their team. The team with the most cones turned over within a set time, eg: 30 seconds, wins. The game can be repeated by lengthening the time, travelling in a specific way (eg: hopping), or having an uneven split of cones to start with.

Torches and tealights

Divide the group into two teams. Line them up across the middle of the hall, facing each other at about a metre apart. One team are the "torches" and the other team are the "tea lights". Call either of the team names. If you call "torches", the torches must chase the tea lights and try to catch them before they reach the wall on their side of the room. Similarly, if you call "tea lights", they try to catch the torches.

Anyone who is caught has to join the other side; then the teams line up again for a second round. You can add excitement by using a prolonged/repeated "T" or by saying other words that begin with "T", before saying either "torches" or "tea lights".

Leading light

Have everyone sit in a circle; then send a volunteer out of the room. Elect a leader to act in a distinct way that everyone can copy (eg: patting their head, yawning, blinking rapidly...). At any time the leader can change the action and everyone else must follow.

When the volunteer comes back into the room, they should stand in the circle to watch everyone as they do the actions. They have to work out who the leader is by watching the group. They have three guesses.

In the dark

Gear
▶ Toilet paper

Divide the group into teams. Give each team enough toilet paper in which to wrap one person from head to toe. The teams must race to be the first to wrap someone within a set time. Judge the winner when the time is up.

Blinded

Gear
▶ 4 buckets
▶ 4 chairs
▶ Large spoon / ladle
▶ Cotton-wool balls
▶ 2 blindfolds (eg: scarves or airline sleep masks)

Line up the children in two teams. Set up two chairs in front of each team, about 2 metres apart. Place a bucket on each chair. In two buckets, place all of the cotton-wool balls. Blindfold the first player from each team. Stand them in front of the chair with the cotton wool and place the large spoon in one of their hands.

They must keep their other hand behind their back. They have a set time (eg: 1 minute) to try and transport the balls to the other bucket. Then the next in line needs to be blindfolded and go. Continue until all the cotton wool has been transported.

Squeak piggy squeak

Gear
▶ Scarf or airline sleep mask

Have the children sit in a circle. Blindfold one of the children and spin them around until disoriented, then get them to walk around the circle until choosing an occupied seat to stop at. After stopping, the blindfolded player sits on the lap of the seated individual and says, "Squeak, Piggy, Squeak" and the person must then squeak like a pig. The blindfolded person must guess who is the squeaker is and, if they guess correctly, the two people switch roles. Now the squeaker becomes the blindfolded player and the game continues. If the person guesses incorrectly, then they are sent back around for another try.

SQUEAK SQUEAK

Lightwork draw-a-word

Gear
▶ Paper
▶ Pens or pencils
▶ A list of different light sources eg: bulb, sun, torch/flashlight...

Split children into teams. One volunteer from each team is shown a word from the list that they must draw—without speech, acting or symbols. When the team works it out, another team member must come up and collect the next word. To make it harder—and more entertaining—the artist could be blindfolded.

Who am I?

Gear
▶ Sticky labels with names of celebrities on eg: Woody Woodpecker, Hannah Montana, The Queen etc.

1. Stick a label on the back of each participant.

2. The participants then go around the room trying to guess who they are. They may only ask questions with "Yes" or "No" as answers.

This game is useful for introducing the question "Who is Jesus?" and the answer that He is the light of the world.

Leading a small group—notes for leaders

- Sit the children in a circle.

Ice-breaker:

- Start by introducing yourself and maybe say your favourite chocolate bar / colour / food.

- Ask children to do the same.

- Ask them what they have liked best so far today… and maybe share with them your favourite bit too!

Fun sheet:

- Explain that we are going to be thinking about the story we just heard.

- Give out a sheet each and pencil or felt-tip pen. Ask them to write their name on the sheet.

- Work through the questions one at a time, using the attached notes to help you. Encourage the children to talk about each question together, rather than racing ahead.

- Encourage them to complete the colouring and puzzle on the back at home. If they are coming to another event at church, or are a member of a weekly church club, then ask them to bring the sheet back and show you.

Memory verse:

If you have extra time at the end of the sheet, remind the children of the memory verse: "The Lord is my light and my salvation." Psalm 27 v 1a

There are a number of ways that you can practise the memory verse:

- Start small, build up
- Use actions or have pictures/symbols instead of, or as well as, words
- Jigsaw puzzle or a code
- Word-cards / balloons (could mix order)—gradually take away or pop balloons
- March it / clap it
- Rap or song

Notes on questions for 4-7s (Reception to Year 2)

1. Who's in charge of the world we live in? Why?

Question 1 is pretty straightforward. So, once they have written "God", ask the children to think about how they can show He's in charge, eg: how can they listen to Him and obey Him?

2. If someone is in charge, how do we treat them?

For question 2 the pictures are:
- an ear (listen)
- someone bowing (respect)
- funny face (being cheeky)
- cheering (celebrating the person)
- hands over ears (ignoring)

Link back afterwards to question 1 and point out that we often do the last (ignore) with regards to God—we forget about Him.

3. Adam and Eve ignored and disobeyed God. Draw one way in which you do the same:

Remind the children what Adam and Eve had done wrong. Then point out that even though we may not be exactly the same, we do still do wrong things…AND think wrong things… AND say wrong things… AND disobey God… and so we deserve to be punished by God.

After they have drawn their answer, explain how these things make God sad because He *is* King. It makes Him angry that we are selfish, and hurt each other, and make a mess of His world.

4. What happens at home or school if you break rules?

When we disobey our teachers/parents, they punish us because we deserve it—and it's the same for God. It wouldn't be fair if God just said: "It doesn't matter", when we do something unkind to someone. And it wouldn't be right if He said: "It doesn't matter" when we treat Him as if He isn't the King. God is the King and in charge, and it is very wrong of us to pretend that He's not the King by disobeying Him.

5. When we ask God to forgive us, what happens to the things that cut us off from God? Can you draw that?

You may find it useful to have some props—either drawn on paper or made of lego—to show that the wrong things we do cut us off from God. Then you can rip up or knock down the wall to show the result of Jesus' death. Ask them what now gets in the way between people and God. (Nothing) Explain that this is a gift they can ask for, a gift they can receive.

Notes on questions for 7-9s (Years 3 and 4)

1. **At the beginning of the story, we saw that God is in charge as He created the world. Think of different words to describe Him.**
Remind the group that God made everything out of nothing, before thinking about question 1. Look to pull out of the group words like "amazing", "powerful", "perfect", "in charge", "wise", "eternal", "loving" etc.

2. **If someone is in charge, how do we treat them?**
Ask how we treat kings, or important people who are in charge, like teachers. (Obey them / listen to them etc.) Then ask about God—give some examples of how we can listen to Him or ignore Him and forget about Him.

3. **Adam and Eve ignored and disobeyed God. Write or draw one way in which you do the same:**
Remind the children what Adam and Eve had done wrong. Then point out that even though we may not be exactly the same, we do still do wrong things…AND think wrong things… AND say wrong things… AND disobey God… and so we deserve to be punished by God. After they have given their answer, explain how these things make God sad because He is King. It makes Him angry that we are selfish, and hurt each other, and make a mess of His world.

4. **How does God punish us? Is that fair?**
When we disobey our teachers/parents, they punish us because we deserve it—and it's the same for God. It wouldn't be fair if God just said: "It doesn't matter", when we do something unkind to someone. And it wouldn't be right if He said: "It doesn't matter" when we treat Him as if He isn't the King. God *is* the King and in charge, and it is very wrong of us to pretend that He's not the King by disobeying Him.

5. **Why did Jesus die and rise again?**
You may find it useful to have some props. Eg: have a load of rubble on the palm of your hand. Talk about how each time we do something wrong, say something wrong, think something wrong or reject God as King—it's as if the pile adds up—and we deserve to be punished for it. However when Jesus, the perfect one, died, He took all our sin onto Himself and therefore our punishment—now transfer the rubble onto your clean palm. Explain that by rising again, Jesus proved to us He was God and death had been beaten. Because of His sacrifice, we can not only be forgiven, but also know we have a place in heaven.

6. **How can you be a "lightbuster" (friends with God)?**
   - [ ] **Walk around with a torch/flashlight**
   - [ ] **Be good all the time**
   - [ ] **Trust in Jesus' death. Say sorry for not living God's way.**

Use question 6 to check that the children really understand what it means to become a Christian, and to look for any misconceptions (eg: being good earns us salvation).

Notes on questions for 9-11s (Years 5 and 6)

1. **How do we know that God is perfect, powerful and in charge? Think back to the story and come up with as many ways as possible.**
Go over the story, focusing on the main points of creation, God's reaction to our sin and the punishment we deserve, Jesus' life and death, and the choice He offers us.

2. **Can you think of ways you put yourself in charge instead of God?**
Ask how we treat kings, or important people in charge, like teachers. (Obey them / listen to them etc.) Then ask about God—we can listen to Him yet often ignore Him and forget about Him. Ask them to jot down ways in which they know they do that. After they have written their answer, explain how it makes God sad because He is King and it makes Him angry that we are selfish, and hurt each other, and make a mess of His world.

3. **What will happen to us because of our attitude against God? Is it fair?**
When we disobey our teachers/parents, they punish us because we deserve it—and it's the same for God. It wouldn't be fair if God said: "It doesn't matter" when we do something unkind. It wouldn't be right if He said: "It doesn't matter" when we treat Him as if He isn't the King. God *is* the King and it is very wrong to pretend that He's not the King by disobeying Him.

4. **Why did Jesus die and rise again?**
You may find it useful to have some props. Eg: have a load of rubble on the palm of your hand. Talk about how each time we do something wrong, say something wrong, think something wrong or reject God as King—it's as if the pile adds up—and we deserve to be punished for it. However when Jesus, the perfect one, died, He took all our sin onto Himself and therefore our punishment—now transfer the rubble onto your clean palm. Explain that by rising again, Jesus proved to us He was God and death had been beaten. Because of His sacrifice, we can not only be forgiven, but also know we have a place in heaven.

5. **How can we accept Jesus' invitation to be His friend? Have you done this?**
Offer a sweet to someone, then ask what they have to do to make it their own. They have to take it—it's no good just looking at it or knowing about it; they need to accept it. Use this sweet illustration to discuss question 5. Go through ways of accepting Jesus' invitation to be His friend and how we can start living with Jesus as our King:

   1. Say "sorry" to God for not treating Him as your King.
   2. Say "thank you" to God for sending Jesus to die so that you can be forgiven.
   3. Ask God to please forgive you, and help you to live with Jesus as your King. You can trust Jesus.

6. **How can we be "lightbusters" and follow Jesus' example?**
Use question 6 to check that the children really understand what it means to become a Christian, and to look for any misconceptions (eg: being good earns us salvation). Talk about how it can be really hard following God—but it's worth it as being His friend lasts for ever. It will help if we remind ourselves how good God is and how He's always kept His promises, as well as asking others to pray.

ONE DAY WONDERS

LIGHTBUSTERS

The Lord is my light and my salvation.
Psalm 27 v 1a

1. Who's in charge of the world we live in? Why?

2. If someone is in charge, how do we treat them?

3. Adam and Eve ignored and disobeyed God. Draw one way in which you do the same.

4. What happens at home or school if you break rules?

5. When we ask God to forgive us, what happens to the things that cut us off from God? Can you draw that?

LIGHTBUSTERS

Jesus died on a wooden cross. But He didn't stay dead! God brought Jesus back to life.

Colour in the squares with a star in them. ➡

LIGHTBUSTERS

The Lord is my light and my salvation.
Psalm 27 v 1a

1. At the beginning of the story, we saw that God is in charge because He created the world. Think of different words to describe Him.

2. If someone is in charge, how do we treat them?

3. Adam and Eve ignored and disobeyed God. Write or draw one way in which you do the same.

4. How does God punish us? Is that fair?

5. Why did Jesus die and rise again?

6. How can you be a "lightbuster" (friends with God)?

   ☐ Walk around with a torch

   ☐ Be good all the time

   ☐ Say sorry for not living God's way and trust in Jesus' death.

LIGHTBUSTERS

Jesus said, "I **am** the **light** of the **world. Whoever follows** me will **never walk** in **darkness**, but **will** have the **light** of **life**."

John 8 v 12

→ Find the **bold** words in the wordsearch. Some are diagonal - or backwards!

D	S	O	R	E	V	E	O	H	W
A	W	A	L	K	W	A	M	E	S
R	W	C	T	H	G	I	L	R	W
K	J	O	A	N	B	E	E	L	O
N	E	I	R	G	H	V	L	T	L
E	S	B	U	L	E	W	I	L	L
S	U	S	T	N	D	E	F	R	O
S	S	L	I	G	H	T	E	S	F

Now copy the left-over letters (in order) to find out who said these words.

— —

"Lightbusters" are friends with God. Jesus came so that the dark things in our life (our sin) can be forgiven. Anyone who trusts in Jesus' death can be friends with God and live with Him for ever.

ONE DAY WONDERS

LIGHTBUSTERS

The Lord is my light and my salvation.
Psalm 27 v 1a

1. How do we know that God is perfect, powerful and in charge? Think back to the story and come up with as many ways as possible.

2. Can you think of ways you put yourself in charge instead of God?

3. What will happen to us because of our attitude against God? Is it fair?

4. Why did Jesus die and rise again?

5. How can we accept Jesus' invitation to be His friend? Have you done this?

6. How can we be "lightbusters" and follow Jesus' example?

LIGHTBUSTERS

Not my fault!

Adam and Eve disobeyed God. They ate fruit from the tree He told them not to eat from. These "snapshots" show what happened next. Copy each picture into the right box.

1. Adam and Eve hid from God among the **trees**.

2. Adam **blames** Eve. Eve **blames** the snake.

3. The **snake** is cursed by God, and will be hated by people.

4. God says **Eve** will now have great pain when she gives birth to children.

5. God says Adam will have to **work** very hard to grow enough food to eat.

6. They are banned from the garden. A flaming **sword** keeps them away from the tree of life.

But God says something surprising to the snake. Cross out the **X**'s to see what it was.

**XHXERXOFXFSXPXRINXXGWXILXL
CXRUXSHXYOXURXHXEAXDX**

_ _ _   _ _ _ _ _ _ _ _

_ _ _ _   _ _ _ _ _

_ _ _   _ _ _ _

It sounds odd doesn't it? But God is promising that one of Eve's family (her offspring) will beat the devil (the snake). This promise is actually all about Jesus! He came as our Rescuer to beat the problem of sin for ever.

You can read this story for yourself in Genesis 3 v 8-15.

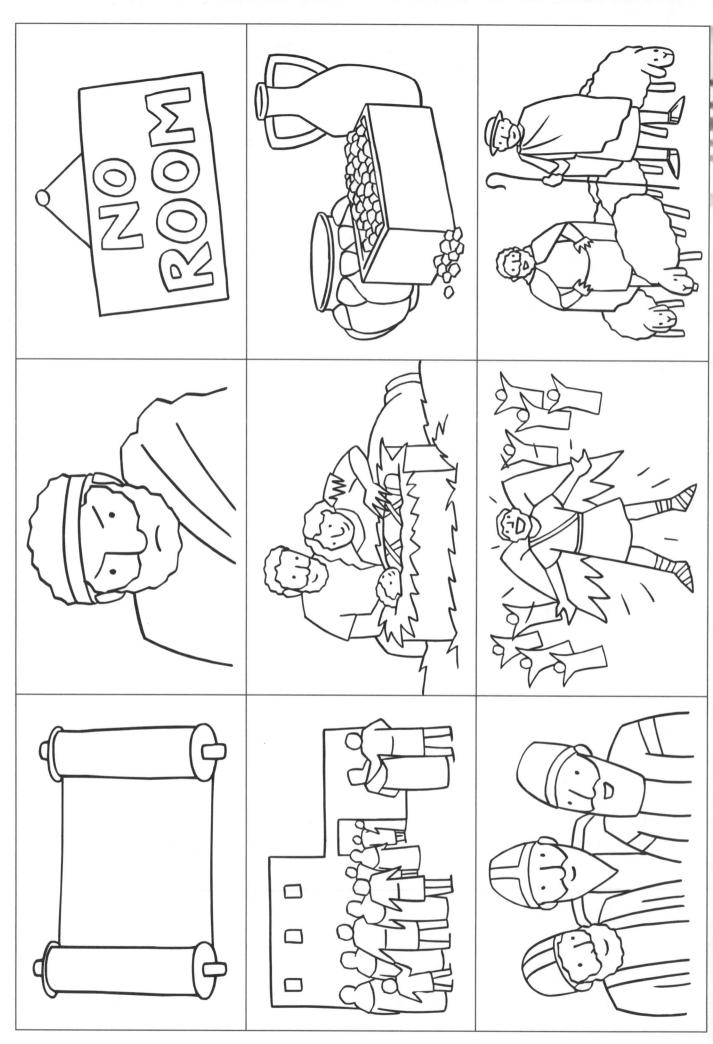

ONE DAY WONDERS

ONE DAY WONDERS

Nativity Signature Bingo

Get a signature in each box. No one can sign your sheet more than three times.

Someone who has a dog	Someone who is wearing red	Someone who loves brussel sprouts	Someone who knows how to sail a boat
Someone who hasn't bought any Christmas presents yet	Someone who is taller than you	Someone with blond hair	Someone who has never been on an airplane
Someone who loves peanut butter	Someone whose name begins with "J"	Someone who can play the piano	Someone who has the same favourite Christmas Carol as you
Someone with laces on their shoes	Someone who is eight years old	Someone with an older brother	Someone who can do a handstand

ONE DAY WONDERS

For Christ died for sins once for all, the righteous for the unrighteous, to bring you to God.

1 Peter 3v18

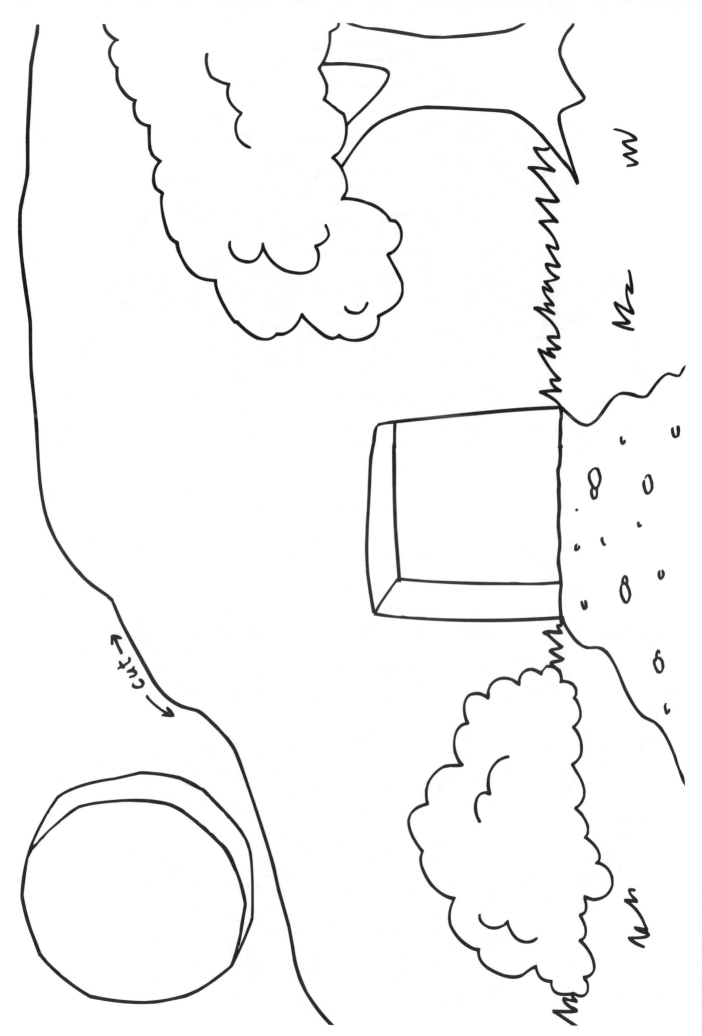

CUT

ONE DAY WONDERS

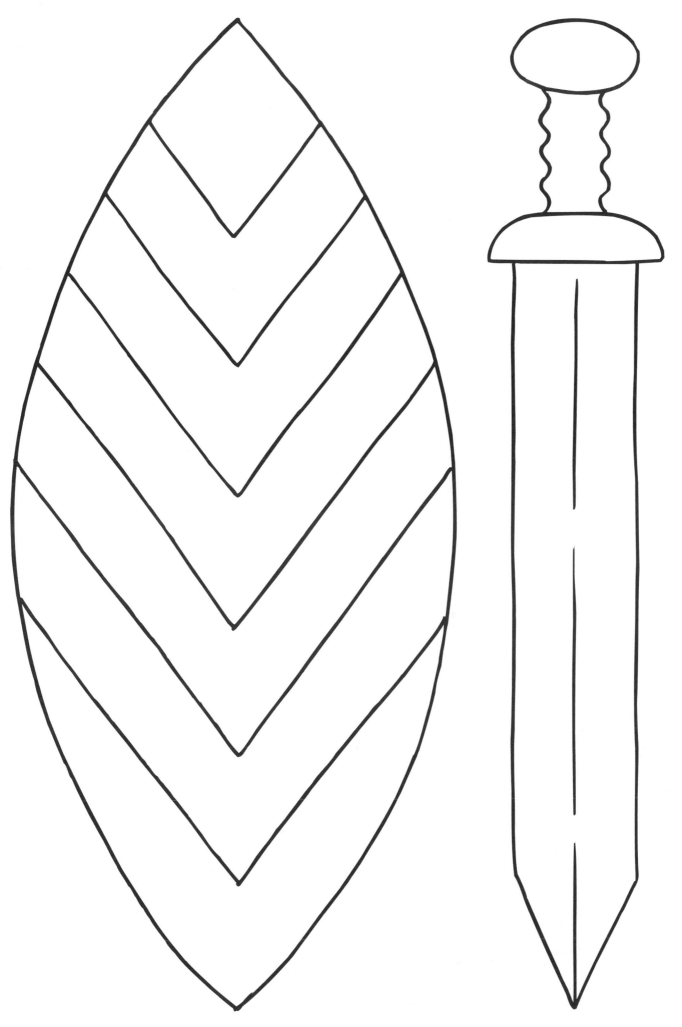

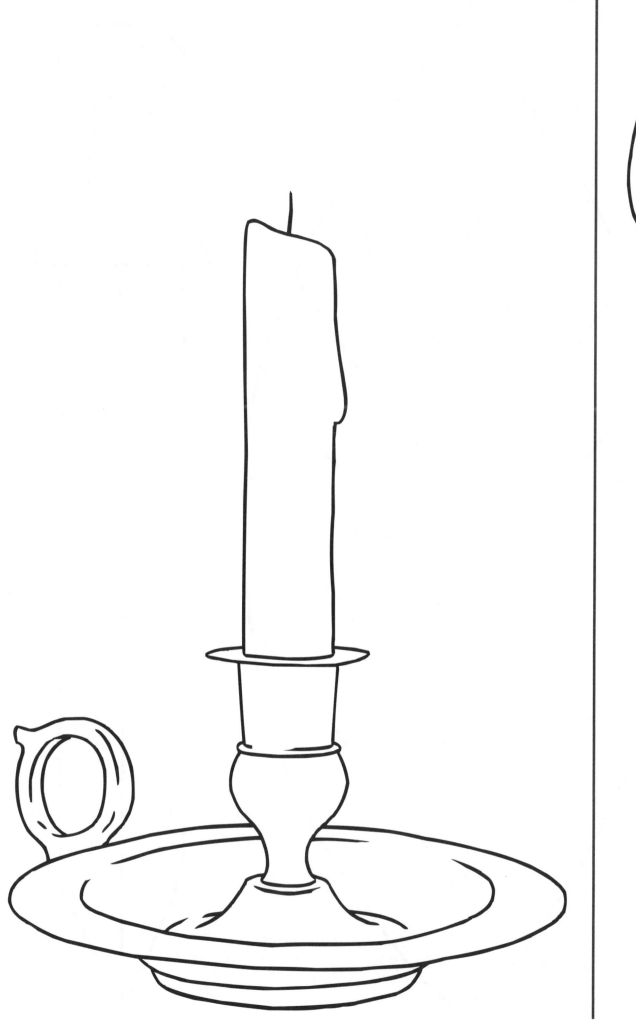

ONE DAY WONDERS

ONE DAY WONDERS

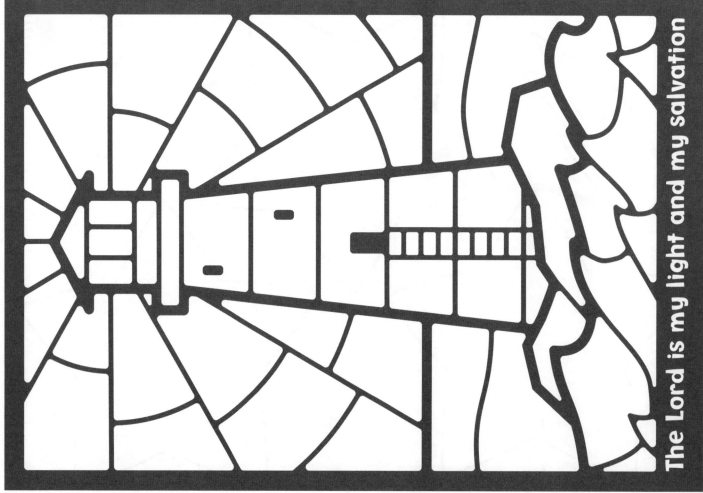

ONE DAY WONDERS

The Lord is my light and my salvation

The Lord is my light and my salvation

# RESOURCES

Leaflets to support your events

At the end of your event, why not give each child or family a themed leaflet to take away with them?

- Each leaflet contains Bible passages, puzzles and questions.

- Suitable for 7-11s to use on their own, or for younger children with help from their parents.

- Also great to give out in church if your event is linked to a church service on the same theme.

Christmas

Easter

Halloween

Fantastic ways to learn memory verses

"I have hidden your word in my heart that I might not sin against you." Psalm 119 v 11

Each event in **One Day Wonders** has a linked memory verse so that each child can go away with some of God's living Word in their heart. **Remember Remember** is packed with creative ways to help children memorise the Bible. These ideas will be ideal for the memory verses learned during your event. **Remember Remember** will also be a great resource for the regular teaching in your church or group.

The above resources are available from:	UK:	www.thegoodbook.co.uk
	N America:	www.thegoodbook.com
	Australia:	www.thegoodbook.com.au

the good book COMPANY

CLICK teaching material

CLICK has a "Biblical Theology" framework, which means it teaches "little stories" as part of the "Big Story" of the Bible.

- Each unit of ten sessions is linked together (often from one book of the Bible).

- These links are reinforced by full-colour teacher's posters and child components.

- The key teaching point of a unit (this is often the key teaching point of the Bible book the unit is based on) will be reinforced each week, so that children remember and understand it.

CLICK is suitable for church groups, mid-week groups and after-school clubs. **CLICK** material will help you teach the Bible faithfully and effectively to the children in your group. It is easy to use and covers three age groups: 3-5s, 5-7s & 8-11s. The sample pack available will allow you to review the whole syllabus and see examples of the child components before you commit to using it with your group.

CLICK is only available from our UK website:
www.thegoodbook.co.uk/click

ONE DAY WONDERS AUTHOR: TAMAR POLLARD

Tamar is the children and schools worker at Highfields Church in Cardiff, having formerly worked as a primary school teacher in Derbyshire. She has been teaching the Bible to children for nearly 20 years. *One Day Wonders* is her first book for The Good Book Company.

SERIES EDITOR: ALISON MITCHELL

Alison is the children's editor at The Good Book Company, where she has written a range of Bible-reading notes for children and families, as well as editing CLICK teaching material. Alison is also involved with training events around the country for children's and youth leaders.